Through Thick and Thin

Through Thick and Thin

*One Foster Family's
Eating Disorder Journey*

CAROLYN ROY-BORNSTEIN

Toplight

Jefferson, North Carolina

To protect the privacy of the individuals,
names of some people and places have been changed.

ISBN (print) 978-1-4766-8731-5 ∞
ISBN (ebook) 978-1-4766-4513-1

LIBRARY OF CONGRESS AND BRITISH LIBRARY
CATALOGUING DATA ARE AVAILABLE

Front cover image © 2021 PopTika/Shutterstock

Printed in the United States of America

Toplight is an imprint of McFarland & Company, Inc., Publishers

Box 611, Jefferson, North Carolina 28640
www.toplightbooks.com

To Janine and Mariah.
Thank you for allowing me to tell our story.
And mostly, thank you for being in my life.

Acknowledgments

I am grateful to my editor Susan Kilby and everyone at McFarland for taking a chance on this book and on me. Thank you also to Roberta Zeff at the *New York Times* and Sylvia Chan at *Entropy* for first publishing essays on the themes and ideas on which this book was built. I am deeply grateful to my writing group and my dear friends Shelley Carpenter, Margaret Flaherty and Lisa Mahoney who read more embryonic versions of this project over the years with diligence and generosity. To all my children, Dan, Neil, Mariah and Janine, you are my lights and my love. And to Saul, you are the best partner anyone could ever have. Thank you for saying yes.

Table of Contents

Table of Contents

SECTION I

In the Beginning

Prologue

I slammed on my brakes, crossing multiple white lines, trying desperately to get to the breakdown lane. Cars careened wildly to avoid us on the rain-slicked highway. Drivers laid on their horns. The dome light snapped on. The passenger door opened.

"Janine, don't!" I screamed, giving the wheel a final wild turn. I heard her seat belt click open. I grabbed her jacket with my right hand as I screeched to a halt, half on and half off the exit ramp. Her head jerked forward then back. I wrenched my body to face her and used my left hand to throw the car into park. Traffic veered around us. Horns blared. I adjusted my reach, trying to include her thin body in my grip, not just her clothes, but my own seat belt was tethering me in place. If I let go of her to unhook it, she'd be gone.

The distance between us grew incrementally. I heard myself screaming. She didn't make a sound. Just inched her 90-pound body out of my car. First one foot out the door. Then the other.

This is how I will lose her, I thought. *This is how she will die.*

I was sobbing now. "Please, Janine. Don't leave me."

I heard sirens in the distance. The police were on their way. *Please hurry.*

I heard her jacket rip. Her weight suddenly not there.

I am too late, I thought.

She was gone.

ONE

A Loving Leap of Faith

"Empty nests are over-rated," I joked. But this was no laughing matter. It was early September. I was sitting at the kitchen table across from my husband Saul, our hands enmeshed, having a serious discussion about whether to become foster parents to two teenage girls, ages 14 and 16, both patients in my pediatric practice.

I had known the girls for seven years, since the day their mother Linda had burst into my practice, unannounced, with no appointment—they weren't even my patients yet—and demanded that I see her daughter Mariah.

"She's not well! You have to help her!" Linda bawled. She shoved Mariah toward me, her younger daughter Janine clutched to her chest.

Mariah looked sick. Her alabaster skin was bloodless. Her dark hair framed her round face, apple cheeks gone pale. She was nine years old, feverish, trembling, and lethargic. Her mother told me her temperature at home had reached 106 degrees and she'd had a shaking chill, or perhaps a seizure, in the bathtub. She had just been seen at the emergency room of the hospital next door to my office. Blood cultures had been drawn and antibiotics prescribed, and she had been discharged home.

But instead of going home, they came here. Linda wanted something else done. Something more. Something now.

"You've got to help her!" she shrieked at me again. Linda was short but she managed to insert her body between her daughter and me, her short hair sticking out from under her purple cloche, her face flushed with desperation as she looked up into mine.

I stayed calm, assuring her I would take care of her child. I gave Mariah an intramuscular injection of a potent antibiotic and hospitalized her while we waited for the culture results. Sure enough, the next day, Mariah's blood culture was growing a rare bacterium: *Haemophilus influenza* or *H flu.*

"You saved her life," Linda told me breathlessly as she flung her arms around me the next day when I rounded on the family at the hospital.

"I'm just doing my job," I said into her hair. The girls had been my patients ever since.

I met the rest of the family in time. Their dad Jimmy brought the girls in as often as Linda. He was usually dressed casually in jeans and flannel coming straight from one of his jobs. He worked full time at Malden Mills, a local company that made polar fleece outerwear. He also worked the register and stocked shelves at a local liquor store part time. It was obvious to me that the girls were the apples of his eye. He puffed with pride as he talked about them, smiling beneath his thick black mustache. I remember once, when Mariah was nearing puberty, having a conversation with Jimmy about her upcoming menses. He rolled his eyes, laughed and said, "I just know what Linda is like at her time of the month. Imagine me when all three of them have their periods?" to which I could not help but lower my eyes and smile.

Jimmy was a cancer survivor. He had had bladder cancer but he had beaten it. He was proud of that fact. That something had tried to take him down and failed. He told me the story of being a survivor on the very first day we met. Next to being a father, it was how he defined himself. His eyes shone as he spoke. His jet-black hair gave him a youthful look that belied all he'd been through.

I remained the girls' pediatrician for the next several years, seeing them through the usual childhood maladies: ear infections, allergic reactions, muscle sprains. Then, the unimaginable happened. Jimmy's cancer came back with metastasis to his lungs. He started treatment; his prognosis was not good.

I tried to help the family as best I could. I attempted to get Jimmy into hospice care. His oncologist stubbornly refused to fill out the paperwork. I referred Linda to a domestic violence shelter one night when the high dose steroids Jimmy was on made him violently psychotic. I got the girls into a support group for children whose parents had cancer.

This time, Jimmy did not survive his illness.

He died the day after Mariah's 12th birthday.

After her husband's death, Linda succumbed to her terrible grief and her own demons. I would learn later from the girls that she started drinking heavily again, even more than she did when she first learned that his cancer was back. She could be violent and cruel.

The Department of Children and Families took the girls away and they spent the next several years in a dizzying series of foster homes and residential programs. They each resorted to physical, self-destructive means of trying desperately to control their rapidly disintegrating world. Mariah started cutting herself, narrowing her pain to thin lines of blood on her wrists. Janine developed anorexia nervosa, severely restricting her food intake and secretly and obsessively exercising. I remember her last foster mother bringing Janine into my office, concerned that she was not eating.

"She's on the treadmill in the middle of the night," she told me. "I hear her."

"I am not," Janine argued indignantly. She could barely keep her eyes open and she wobbled when she tried to stand, she was so dehydrated. I sent her to emergency room for IV fluids to stabilize her. From there she went to her first eating disorder program, starting down the long road of anorexia treatment.

Mariah was able to finally gain control of her self-injurious behavior. She stopped cutting. She ended up in a stable foster home for the next couple of years with a lovely older woman named Hannah.

Janine was less fortunate. She spent several years in various treatment programs—most of them close to her hometown of Hillsboro. The last one was a prolonged stint in a facility called Hope Village which specializes in emotional and behavior problems but not specifically eating disorders. Its Clinton Care campus was in a suburb west of Boston, more than an hour from her family, her friends, her last foster home, her social worker, and me. As her pediatrician, I tried to stay involved, asking her case worker for updates regularly.

After several months, the worker stopped returning my phone calls. So did her supervisor.

And that was how I lost track of Janine.

One day the girls' court appointed special advocate or CASA worker, Michelle, called me at work. Every six months, CASA had to prepare a report for the judge, basically making sure kids were up to date with their check-ups, immunizations and dental visits. I told her Mariah was up to date with her shots and check-ups though I hadn't seen her in a while.

Then I took a chance.

"Can I ask you for an update on Janine?" I asked. "Her social worker stopped returning my calls." I wasn't sure what the rules of privacy would be. Was I even Janine's pediatrician anymore? She'd been in the program for almost a year. Another pediatrician—an adolescent specialist from Children's Hospital—was her provider of record now.

Michelle obliged. She started with a long, dispirited sigh. I could almost see her shaking her head as she spoke.

"She's not good," she told me. Apparently, Janine's previous foster family was deemed by DCF to be incapable of providing the intensive care and supervision Janine's eating disorder would require. And while Janine's grandmother was attending the twice-a-month family therapy sessions that Clinton Care required, placement with her was also unrealistic. Janine was stuck. With no home to go to and her mother unable to care for her, she was unmotivated to get well.

"She'll go all day long without eating," Michelle said sadly in her thick Midwestern twang.

I swallowed hard as I took in this information. I pictured Janine sitting alone on a bed, starving herself, her once bright blue eyes blank with hunger, healthy brown curls now lifeless and dry.

"I haven't seen Mariah in a while, Michelle. Everything okay there?" I asked. I assumed she was still in Hannah's home. I was wrong. It turned out that Hannah's aging parents were requiring more of her time. Her grown daughter was pregnant and was moving back in. Feeling overwhelmed with her own family obligations, she had sadly asked DCF to find Mariah a new foster home. Apparently, the new home wasn't working out.

Section I—In the Beginning

"She's been there three weeks," Michelle said. "She won't even unpack her bags."

My heart broke for these girls. They didn't deserve any of this—losing their dad at such a young age, a mother too ill herself to care for them, a revolving door of programs and foster homes. That night, after my staff had gone home for the evening, I sat alone with my thoughts for a long time. I can't say why these girls touched me so deeply. I had been a pediatrician for decades and a nurse ten years before that. I'd heard stories like theirs before, witnessed equal tragedy in other families. But these girls brought out something in me that no other patient ever had. I cared for them as their doctor, sure. But I wanted to do more. I felt an urge to reach out. To offer help in some way to these girls who had no one. To perhaps be the mother their own could not be right now.

I told Saul the whole story. He knew vaguely about this family. I talked in detail-less terms about my days at work with him over dinner and in bed at night. Now he was learning their names, their ages and new details about their sad situations. Now I was coming to him asking him to make them part of our family. They had only one parent left and a fragile one at that. This could be a very long-term commitment and I wanted him fully aware of this, going in with eyes wide open.

He gripped my hands firmly in his, nodding. His forehead wrinkled in vicarious pain. He met my gaze across the table.

"Call DCF," he said. "Tell them yes."

So I did.

But not the next day. Or the following day. Or even the day after that. I came home from work night after night to Saul asking, "So did you call them today?" eager as a puppy. Once he had made up his mind that he was going to open his home to these girls, he was anxious to get the process started. I, on the other hand, seemed to be developing a serious case of cold feet.

I had already checked off the larger boxes. We'd consulted with both of our grown sons before moving forward. They lived close by, Dan in Maine, Neil in New Hampshire. Both were in committed relationships. Neither had spent a night at their old home in years, preferring to drive the relatively short distances after a visit with us to be with their significant others. In answer to my question "Are you okay if Dad and I do this?" Neil and Dan had both laughed and said, "Why would we mind?" But we wanted them to know that their old rooms were going to be occupied by two teenage girls. Giving away their bedrooms felt like a no-going-back move and I wanted everyone on board.

With the larger boxes checked, I began to worry about smaller things. This would be starting all over again for me and Saul. Packing lunches, catching school buses, making sure homework was completed. I had done all that before, of course. But now I was older. How would I hold up day after day? I focused on things that might be different with the girls. Would they confide in me about their relationships with boys? Would I know what to say? From there, I turned to true minutiae. Would it be awkward walking around in my pajamas in front of two young ladies who used to be my patients?

I had readied everyone around me for this new commitment— this loving leap of faith. But now I was coming to realize that the one person who might not be ready was me. I knew that DCF was desperate. There were only so many foster homes in Hillsboro. The girls had already each inhabited many of them. They were keeping Mariah in one where she wasn't happy. Surely Janine's situation required specialized training. They were running out of options. Was I really up for this? Had I jumped the gun? Or worse, did I believe on some level that Saul would not go for this idea of opening up our comfortably empty nest to two new and needy teens? Did I think that by magnanimously making the offer, I could assume the role of the good guy? *I would have raised them, but Saul said no.*

But Saul had not said no. In fact, he had specifically said, "We have to do this, Carolyn. We have the chance to do something good here, and if we don't, we'll regret it for the rest of our lives." I was somewhat taken aback by his unwavering enthusiasm right out of the gate and a little unnerved by my lack of the same.

One of the things I have to do as a pediatrician is talk to pregnant teens about their options. We talk about keeping the baby, having an abortion, or giving the child up for adoption. I tell them that this will be one of the hardest decisions they will ever have to make. That no matter what they decide, there may be days when they wake with regret. If they have an abortion, they may have moments when they wonder what their lives would be like with a child. If they had a baby, that would be hard too, and there may be times when they question their choice. Would it be the same for me? Would I regret, like Saul predicted, not doing this if we decided not to take the girls in? On the other hand, if we went ahead with it, would there be days when raising teenage girls would make us second guess our decision?

I eventually did call DCF. If Saul could commit to this giant unknown, so could I. As the days ticked on, my resolve strengthened; my choice felt clear and my own. I grew excited and determined about this next chapter in our lives.

The conversation did not go as I expected. With Janine so ill and so far from discharge, I assumed we would take Mariah first—get her out of the foster home that was making her miserable—then, when Janine was ready for discharge, we would take her, too.

"Forget about Mariah," Syd Reynolds, the girls' social worker told me bluntly. "Mariah's fine. Just focus on Janine." From what Michelle had told me, Mariah sounded anything but fine. But Janine did sound worse. She had given up all hope of discharge. "I might as well live in a dumpster like a piece of trash," Syd said she had told her therapist. "I might as well be dead."

The following week Syd sat down with Janine and her therapist Ben and together they broached the subject of coming to live with us.

"Janine, your pediatrician and her husband have come forward and would like you to consider allowing them to be your foster parents," he said.

Sitting at home, I pictured worst case scenarios: Janine shutting down. Not open to the idea. Suspicious. Janine flatly rejecting us. Janine too weak and sick to even register what was being put on the table.

None of that happened. Syd told me she saw a small smile on Janine's face for the first time in a very long time. Janine in fact readily turned her focus to practical matters. "Well, I can't keep calling her Dr. Bornstein now, can I? That would just be awkward," she noted. "And I'll have to have a new pediatrician if she's my foster mother. Because that would be too weird if my foster mother were my doctor, too."

She also immediately started advocating for herself.

"Can I go to Hillsboro High if I live in Newburyport? I want to go to Hillsboro High."

Despite Janine's initial curiosity and her willingness to at least be open to the idea of us as foster parents, the actual transition would not be as smooth as all that. It would be another ten months before she would come to live with us permanently. Ten months of bi-weekly family therapy with her, visitation at the program, then passes home. Ten months of learning about the disease that had such a stranglehold on this child. Ten months before we would actually become her foster parents. But at this moment, her reaction was as good as we could hope for.

Two

Where Is Home?

While driving to Clinton Care to meet Janine—Saul for the first time—I thought back to that last time I had seen her. Dark circles under her eyes. Too weak to stand. If she had looked that bad at the beginning of anorexia, what must she look like now? In the clutches of it? In residential treatment for it?

We pulled up to Clinton Care not knowing what to expect. We had had a few phone conversations with Janine's therapist Ben, but only so he could let us know that Janine was open to the idea of us. Now that I was actually here, I had butterflies in my stomach. Would she remember me? Would I recognize her? Would she and Saul connect?

We stood on the porch of the program's building and rang the bell. We could hear girls' voices—loud, not unhappy—from within. No one answered. The sun was setting, darkness gathering around us. We rang again. A thin young woman with pulled-back blonde hair, a pierced nose and a tattoo of a spiral staircase climbing her arm answered the door.

"We're here to see Ben," Saul said.

Is she anorexic too? I wondered.

Then she reached behind her back and pulled a walkie-talkie from her waistband and spoke into it.

"Sara, can you cover me in the kitchen? I have to bring some parents down the B staircase."

The staff person introduced herself as Macy and led us down a set of stairs and into a small corner office with no windows.

"He'll be right down," she said and left, leaving the door open. I surveyed the dingy room. A large desk and a worn office chair on wheels occupied most of it. Papers and books littered its surface.

Among the detritus, several photos of bright, beaming toddlers sprouted up like spring crocuses. An old wooden bookcase overflowed with textbooks and ratty paperbacks. A small end table held Day-Glo–colored balls of Play-Doh wrapped in Saran Wrap, a box of sand with a tiny wooden rake in it, and a small plastic basket filled with little stuffed animals, all clearly designed to calm young clients' nerves.

Ben wheezed into the room, looking at his watch, catching his breath.

"Sorry I'm late." He was short in stature with dark curly hair and glasses he regularly pushed back up on the bridge of his nose.

"I'm Ben," he added, needlessly. We held out our hands. His palm was sweaty as we shook it. He sat in his beat-up office chair then gestured toward the pair against the wall. We took our seats.

"So I thought we'd meet together for a little bit before Janine comes down. See if you guys have any questions I can answer."

The truth was we didn't have any questions. Or maybe we had a million.

"We just want to meet her," Saul said.

"Slow down, slow down," Ben said with an exaggerated eye roll. He held up both hands as if to literally block our moving forward, toward our girl. "I've presented you guys as an option for her, but I've left the ball squarely in her court. Like I told you on the phone, Janine tends to be a people-pleaser. I don't want her to feel like she has to say yes to this just because it's what we all want."

Saul and I glanced at each other. I agreed with Ben to a certain extent. We certainly didn't want her to think we were forcing ourselves upon her. On the other hand, I think most 14-year-old children have adults helping them make decisions if not telling them outright what to do. I knew as a pediatrician that when children are in total control with no limits or structure, it can be scary to them, or overwhelming.

I told Ben I wanted other adults (him!) suggesting to her that our home could be a very good place for her. He assured us that he would ... in time.

"Janine did tell her mother about you and Saul on a phone call

13

the other night," Ben told us. "She thinks you're an angel sent from God to save Janine's life. That you saved Mariah's life and now you're going to save Janine, too."

I smiled and shook my head at Linda's dramatic hyperbole.

"Actually, the rumor around Clinton Care is that you saved Janine from malaria," Ben told us. I laughed.

"Well, it was Mariah and it was *H flu*. Other than that...."

Our slowly dying laughter left an awkward silence.

"Well, should I get her?" Ben asked. Saul and I nodded in unison. Ben disappeared into the hall and returned a few minutes later with Janine. My fears evaporated. She was the same sweet smiling girl I remembered. Her curly brown hair framed her face like a painting. Her eyes were the same gleaming blue-sky blue. She was even wearing an outfit I thought I remembered from her days as my patient: ripped jeans and a bright pink plaid button-down shirt. The giant fuzzy koala bear slippers were new to me, of course. She giggled awkwardly and took the chair next to the Play-Doh table, curling her feet underneath her and wrapping a lock of hair nervously around her finger.

The first goal of our meeting was just to get to know each other. Janine talked about all the things she loved. Music. All kinds. Saul told her about his giant collection of vinyl records and the device our boys had bought him that converted vinyl to CDs.

"Even that's obsolete now that everything's gone digital," he commented.

She wanted to learn to play the guitar.

"We have one at the house you could start on," I offered.

"You do?" she asked, wide-eyed.

I nodded and told her how Neil taught me to play and what a patient and kind teacher he was and how he could probably teach her, too. I resisted the urge to show her a picture of "her room" on my phone, where the guitar currently resided. That would *not* be taking it slow.

She told us how she was asked to sing the National Anthem this coming Friday night at the high school football game.

"Wow, that's amazing," Saul said. "How did they know you could sing?"

"A teacher from here recommended me," she told us. When we still looked perplexed, she went on. "We have to sing in the bathroom so that staff knows we're not exercising or vomiting," she explained, not a shred of self-consciousness.

She liked to crochet. I could teach her how to knit! She liked to write. So did I! She'd filled eleven diaries in the nine months she had been at Clinton Care.

"I might write a book someday about all this," she said earnestly.

"Carolyn wrote a book," Saul told her.

"You did?" she asked, turning to me, seeming impressed.

Ben Googled my name on his phone and showed her the book cover. I had written *Crash: A Mother, a Son, and the Journey from Grief to Gratitude* about our family's experience with Neil's traumatic brain injury at the hands of a drunk driver in a crash that killed his girlfriend Trista.

"You're famous!" she cried. I had thought about bringing her a copy of my memoir as a gift—to show her what kind of a "through-thick-and-thin" family we were. But I didn't even know if she was a reader. And then there were Ben's words. "Go slow."

She liked animals. She might want to be a vet.

"I like to do things," she told us. "I like to have adventures and learn things." Saul talked about the Peabody Essex Museum near our home. She thought she'd been there before. The Chinese house sounded familiar. She and Saul agreed it was interesting but that they'd rather have their modern conveniences like beds and toilets.

Finally, Ben brought the conversation to the more germane topic. He wanted Janine to help us understand what it was like having an eating disorder.

"It's one thing to know anorexia as a doctor," he said, looking at me. "It's quite another to live with someone struggling with it."

She told us she was very body conscious. "I hate being called a twig," she said. That seemed counterintuitive to me. After all, wasn't the goal of anorexia to eat and weigh as little as possible? Wouldn't you want people to notice? I guess I had a lot to learn.

"How will Saul and Carolyn know if you're struggling with a meal?" Ben prompted. "What does that look like?"

Janine grew quiet, stared at her koala feet.

"Well," she started, "sometimes my legs will shake. Or I'll just stare off into space. Or sometimes I'll take my sandwich apart. Rip the crust from the bread, tear the stringy ends off the turkey."

She paused.

"Look," she said bluntly, staring us right in the eye. "I can sit here all day long and tell you what it's like to have an eating disorder. But in the moment?" She hesitated. "In the moment, it's not pretty."

My poor, brave girl. Such an act of faith to reveal that chink in her armor.

When we left Clinton Care, a dense fog had settled over the dark neighborhood. Moisture was so thick in the air it coated my arms with mist even though it wasn't raining. Despite the dreariness, I couldn't help but feel optimistic.

"How do you think it went?" I asked Saul, rubbing his shoulder as he drove through the fog.

"I think it went pretty well," he said as he leaned toward the windshield, peering through the murk. "She's a great girl."

And there he was cutting through to the core of it. Despite all her troubling past—her mental illness, living in the system for years—inside was a bright light of potential. And Saul had seen it.

By the end of October, after six weeks of bi-weekly therapy and visiting Janine every weekend, we were finally deemed ready for our first home pass. It was scheduled to occur over Halloween weekend. We were excited and a little nervous at the same time. We grandly and naively planned an entire day: morning at the Boston Science Museum, lunch at our house, then an afternoon at a park near our home that featured an annual Halloween panto.

Ben called the night before the pass, saying Janine had refused dinner because she was so anxious.

"I hope she'll eat breakfast," he said ominously. "She should be done by eight, but you might want to give her a little more time than that." In other words, don't come too early.

When we showed up at Clinton Care at nine, we were told by the staff that Janine was having a hard time with her breakfast. We soon learned that by "having a hard time" they meant that not only had she refused to eat the food, she had also thrown her plates on the floor, left the dining room, and boldly walked into the kitchen which was off-limits to residents. When anorexic teens in the program refuse meals or snacks, they are given bottles of Ensure to drink in their stead. Janine had refused that as well. Then she refused her meds, went up to her room, pulled the covers over her head and refused to speak.

This did not bode well.

The staff led us into the conference room. We took our places in the familiar plastic chairs and waited. For what, we weren't sure. We had heard from Janine and Ben many times about this shutting down behavior. We knew that Janine could be very stubborn. When she decided she was not going to do something (like eat) there was generally no talking her into it. But she had made some breakthroughs recently. It used to be that once something went awry for Janine, she wouldn't eat for the rest of the day. But she'd gotten away from that, intentionally deciding that it didn't have to be that black or white. She could have a rough morning and still eat lunch and dinner.

She'd even been so flexible as to eat her lunch at eleven o'clock in the morning when her school unexpectedly changed their mealtimes. This was huge. Anorexics have very rigid rules for eating and one of Janine's—leftover from accompanying her Auntie Dee to her Weight Watchers meetings when Janine was nine years old—was that at least two hours had to pass between meals and snacks. When she learned of this new mealtime change, her first reaction was "I'm not doing that. I just won't eat lunch." Later she told us that when she got her first eleven o'clock lunch, she just gritted her teeth and forced herself to take that first bite. After that, she was slowly able to complete the meal.

The clock ticked. Minutes turned into an hour. Saul and I had not brought any books or games with us, optimistically expecting to just pick Janine up and be off on our adventure. So we just sat.

Staff members periodically checked in with us.

Section I—In the Beginning

"Can I bring you guys anything?" they asked. "Water?" All we really wanted them to bring to us was Janine.

"Tell her it's okay," I implored them. "Tell her we'll wait."

"Tell her she can take all the time she wants," Saul added. "We understand. Tell her we're not mad."

Each time, they nodded and slipped out of the conference room, shutting the door behind them. Each time we'd wait. Each time, they came back and offered some apology or explanation.

"Sorry, guys. She's really struggling today."

They never asked us to leave. And so, we waited.

Finally, Macy came in and said, "Do you guys want to just visit her here? I think she could handle that."

"Sure!" we both literally jumped up at the opportunity, glad that Janine was even considering meeting with us. Macy disappeared out the door. I paced around the room, looking out the grimy window, dragging my finger through chalk dust on the blackboard, trying to dissipate nervous energy.

Finally, the staff brought Janine in. She slumped into a nearby chair mumbling something about being a hot mess. I put my hand on her shoulder.

"Oh, my girl," I whispered. It's what I used to call her when she was my patient.

We had brought our dog Homer with us thinking all we were doing was picking Janine up. We thought he'd keep her company in the back seat for the long ride.

"Would you like to meet him?" Saul asked her now.

"Yes!" she squealed.

We brought Homer up onto the porch. Janine convinced staff to let him into the foyer. Petting the dog seemed to calm Janine and soon she was cooing into his furry neck. The staff quietly left us alone. The crisis had passed. Saul told Janine what we had planned. The science museum in the morning. *Maudslay Is Haunted* in the afternoon. She perked up. "What's *Maudslay Is Haunted*?" she asked. We described it as best we could: a walk through the forest with timed vignettes and sketches along the way, some scary (or at least weird and eerie), others just amusing or silly.

"That's still possible," Saul said, glancing at the clock on the conference room wall.

"It is?"

"Mmhm."

"Okay, I'll go find staff." With that, she skipped out the door and into the hall, then turned and ran back to us on tiptoe.

"Sorry about this morning," she said.

Saul and I waved her away and smiled at each other. We were proud of Janine for turning herself around like this. Going from a morning of complete refusal to now being open to a first pass. We were proud of ourselves, too. We had hung in there. Relayed messages to Janine of our steadfastness, our resolve. I hoped that her agreeing to come with us was more than just curiosity about a Halloween show. I hoped it was the beginnings of trust.

Saul and I had feared that with her breakfast and med refusal, her pass privileges might be rescinded, but soon staff appeared with a packed lunch and snack for her and an empty food log for us to record her intake. There were forms we were given to sign, a contract basically making us promise to keep her in sight at all times. I wondered if this was wise, sending her out with no breakfast. No fuel in the tank.

I didn't have long to fret. Janine came bopping back into the conference room in thin leggings and a skimpy top. Staff waved good-bye, ready to send her on her way, but we told her it was October and chilly and we insisted she bring a sweater. She rolled her eyes, then ran back to her room to accommodate her overprotective new almost-foster parents.

"We're proud of you, ya know," Saul told her when she came back, newly sweatered. She laughed and rolled her eyes. "You really rallied. You were able to turn yourself around after a really rough start. That's something."

Janine smiled and nodded, as if taking in the compliment. She seemed pleased with herself as she sat in the back of the car with Homer, petting him and getting all furry. We talked back and forth over the music on the radio. We stopped at a pharmacy and bought her some Orajel for a canker sore she showed us. She hadn't told anyone at the program about it. Between the sweater and the canker sore, I realized that we already cared more about Janine than anyone there. She was their client. But she was our family. Or at least we hoped she'd soon be. Although they had known her for ten months, and Saul for six weeks, I'd known her since she was seven. And clearly, she shared things with me that she hadn't with them. Maybe it was just her reverting back to our familiar doctor-patient relationship. Still, I couldn't help feeling special as her confidante.

As we drove around Newburyport, we gave her a little tour. We pointed out the swan fountain in the frog pond behind the brick courthouse in the center of town, the Firehouse Center for the Performing Arts where we would see music and plays, the boardwalk downtown where boats would dock in the summer. I pushed my luck, showing her the high school, "go slow" ringing in my ears.

Then we got to our house. She made her way tentatively around the first floor, through the living room, past the bathroom, then kitchen, then dining room. I followed.

"It goes in a circle like my Nana's," she announced. Yay! Something felt familiar. We went upstairs.

"This is your room," I told her.

"Oh my God! It's so cute!" she exclaimed, flopping on the bed that had been my son's. "This bed is so comfy!" She was speaking in exclamation points now. And though I knew she used "OMG, it's so cute" to describe myriad things—clothes, haircuts, cat videos on social media—it still felt special and encouraging that she was reacting this way to her new home. I pointed to the guitar standing up in the corner of the room. I showed her the book I had used when I first learned to play. We practiced playing E, F, and G on the first string. I could hear Saul preparing lunch downstairs. I wondered if the sound of the clinking glasses and clanging silverware was making her anxious. If it was, she wasn't letting on.

We sat at the dining room table. Janine nibbled at her baby carrots and sipped her 1 percent milk, ignoring her sandwich. We chatted, trying to make her comfortable with small talk. When her carrots and milk were gone, she faced her sandwich. Rather than pick it up to eat, she began lifting off the top, looking underneath.

Making a face. Taking out the cheese and the turkey. Wiping the bread against the rim of her plate, purging the slices of excess mayonnaise. Basically, doing anything except eating the sandwich. Saul and I exchanged anxious glances. He was the one to finally acknowledge the elephant in the room.

"Having a hard time with that sandwich, huh?" he offered gently.

Janine nodded. Saul went into the living room to put on some music, something she'd identified in therapy that could help her through a meal. While he was gone, she whispered to me, "It's really stressful when they don't put my sandwich together correctly."

"That's okay," I told her. "You put it back the right way and that'll make it easier to eat."

We kept up the light conversation, me with one eye on Janine and one on her plate. I watched her eat her bread in tiny cubes, move the meat around her plate, pick at her cheese. By now Homer was at her feet, optimistically anticipating leftovers. Lunch was taking way longer than he was used to. But when do you call it quits? Once again, Saul called the shot.

"Want me to take your plate away, Janine?" She visibly relaxed back in her chair, away from the table.

"Yes. Get it away from me," she said, giving the plate of scraps a tiny shove forward. Food. The enemy. She had eaten most of it, though, and, considering how her day had started—refusing breakfast and meds and Ensure—we weren't exactly displeased. After all, we'd done a better job than staff at helping her to eat, hadn't we? I took pride in that small (or not so small, as I would learn) accomplishment.

While Saul cleared the table, I showed Janine the two skeins of white yarn I'd bought and the hat pattern I'd downloaded from the Internet. We each took a skein and a size F crochet hook and worked side by side on the couch. We each finished two rows.

"How come yours looks so much neater than mine?" she complained.

"Practice," I explained with a wink.

Soon it was time to go to the park. Janine took quite a bit of

Homer-fur off her leggings with a lint brush. I petted the dog while I waited for her.

"The vet says he needs to lose weight," I said, absently. As soon as the words were out of my mouth, I wanted to kick myself. How could I be so stupid? We had learned in therapy that any mention of weight could trigger anxiety in a patient with anorexia. How could I say something so triggering on our first pass home?

"Oh, I don't think he's that chubby," Janine said, working the lint brush. Was she really not bothered by my comment, I wondered, or would we be processing this in therapy with Ben?

I offered Janine the front seat on the way to the park so she wouldn't get her leggings re-Homered. She accepted after the requisite "Are you sure?"

When we got to the park, I was surprised there weren't many cars. *Maudslay Is Haunted* is usually a standing room only event in our town. Also missing were the signs: ghosts and goblins with arrows pointing out the trails. Eventually I realized the problem. I had the wrong day. We had missed it by a week.

Janine tried not to show her disappointment. I swallowed mine as well. Saul had an idea.

"What if we found a haunted house between here and Clinton Care?" he asked.

"Yeah!" she effused. It didn't take us long to settle on Salem, Massachusetts, home of the Salem witch trials and Halloween capital of the world. Or at least New England. Again, I gave Janine the front seat. She reminded me that she needed to eat her snack at 3 o'clock. It was quarter of.

She flipped through stations on the radio. At first, she sang along softly—I could tell she had a good voice—but soon I could see her eyelids drooping in the reflection of her face in the side view mirror. Her head lolled to one side. Poor thing. No dinner, no breakfast and less than a complete meal for lunch. She must have had such a negative energy balance at that point; it was no wonder she was exhausted.

Suddenly Janine's eyes flew open.

"Do you have my snack?"

Two. Where Is Home?

The clock on the radio read exactly three.

In Salem, the streets were packed with Halloween revelers in costume. We pointed out the best costumes to each other: Elvis. Marilyn Monroe. Elvira. We went through the 3-D haunted house with our plastic glasses that made the floor look wavy when it was actually flat. Actors in creepy costumes jumped out and screamed at us or followed us closely with their breath on our necks. One room was pitch black. Stringy things suspended from the ceiling tickled our faces. Saul told me later that Janine had grabbed onto his shirt from behind so he reached his hand behind his back and she took it.

We still had an hour to kill before we had to take her back to Clinton Care, so we decided to go to the Peabody Essex Museum. There was an exhibit called "Beyond Human: Artist-Animal Collaboration." Though it was geared toward younger children, it was perfect for animal-loving Janine. She ooh'ed and ahh'ed at the videos of puppies and kittens. She sat on a fur couch, equipped with a motor that simulated the slow heartbeat of a hibernating polar bear. We watched a short film on bower birds and marveled at how they constructed their huge dome-like homes and decorated them with seeds and berries, like little Buddha offerings. We went through the nature center and tried to guess which birds were stuffed and which were painted decoys. In one of our favorite exhibits, the artist had dipped the feet of beetles and cockroaches into paint and let them walk across the canvas.

"Hmm. Bug art," Janine declared.

Just as it turned five o'clock, as we walked up the steps to Clinton Care, a mother and father were walking down.

"Another one returns home, right?" Saul noted.

"This is not my home," Janine grumbled through clenched teeth.

I wondered what felt like home to her now. Not the program, obviously. Not her last foster home where she couldn't go back. Not the condo where she was taken from her mom. At our house, she had a yellow bedroom with a handmade quilt and a guitar in the corner on which she could now play E, F, and G. I hoped that would feel like home to her soon.

THREE

Insiders

In the treatment of eating disorder, a goal weight range is chosen for the patient by her health care providers based on her past growth curves as well as her ideal body weight. Then, patients have to maintain that weight in order to enjoy certain privileges. For Janine, these privileges included working out at the campus gym a couple of times a week and going on outdoor activities with the other girls. If she dipped below her goal weight, she was placed on what was called "medical protocol." On medical protocol, she had to conserve calories. Her gym and outdoor activities privileges were rescinded. She could no longer walk to school. She even had to take the elevator from the kitchen and common areas up to her dorm room on the second floor. "I have to basically eat and lie down" is how Janine put it.

Also, if Janine was on med protocol, passes home were not allowed.

Ben called us the night before our next therapy session. He told us that Janine had not been doing well since her pass with us—not completely restricting but struggling with meals and snacks. He predicted that by our next session the following evening, she'd be back on med protocol. He said she found our visit stressful. In particular, he said she had found my saying "this is your room" overwhelming.

I felt blamed by Ben. He had admonished us to "go slow" with Janine. Now he seemed to be saying she was suffering the consequences of us moving too fast. Even though she had been struggling with food for years, he seemed to be saying that this latest struggle was because of us. Or at least me.

Or maybe I was blaming myself. I knew in my head I was supposed to go slow. But my heart wanted to plunge in. The high school tour. The "this is your room" comment. I couldn't help myself. I knew this all must be very hard for Janine. It's a lot to ask someone to start all over again in a new foster home. Ours would be the girls' twelfth. I just wanted this all to work out. I wanted Janine home with us. I wanted her to want us as much as we wanted her. Now, if she lost weight and was put on med protocol, I felt it would be all my fault.

When we met with Ben the next night, before he "brought her down," he said that she had in fact maintained her minimum, skin-of-her-teeth weight. She was not (yet) on med protocol. His dire prediction had not come true. I gave a little "yay" in my heart. I was learning to be grateful for every small miracle.

When Janine finally joined us, she seemed subdued. Ben wanted to process the entire visit from beginning to end. He started by pointing out that her anxiety began the Thursday before the pass when she first learned of it. She acknowledged that it *was* anxiety-provoking to think about starting all over again with new foster parents, but in a break from Ben's completely negative interpretation of her reaction, she said it was actually *good* for her to see her room. She used the word "comforting."

"Now I have something real to picture when I think about getting out of here."

I smiled at Janine. I looked at Ben. If he felt betrayed by her comment or mistaken in any way, he didn't let on. He just nodded with arched eyebrows as if this were news to him.

She got quite animated talking about the rest of the day. The haunted house. The Peabody Essex Museum. Crocheting. The guitar. Ben again seemed mildly perplexed by this suddenly positive spin. Was she people-pleasing right now? Or had she genuinely had time to digest her experience and decide that it wasn't so bad after all?

"What made you finally decide to go with the Bornsteins after struggling all morning?" Ben asked her. She was squeezing a pink rubber octopus from the plastic basket of calming toys rhythmically in her hands. First one half of it, then the other would blow up like a frog's rannula. She shrugged.

"I don't know. I guess I figured it was better than sitting around the dorm all day." Great. We were better than a program.

I would take it.

"I had this expectation," she continued, "that I was going to come back to Clinton Care and feel amazing. And if I didn't feel amazing, then that must mean I suck."

"Wait. Wouldn't that mean that Saul and I suck?" I asked.

She giggled, maybe at hearing her pediatrician use the word "suck." I began to realize just how much Janine internalized everything. When things go wrong in Janine's world she automatically blames herself. It's part of the deep self-loathing that provided fertile ground for the development of this eating disorder in the first place. The science isn't entirely clear about which comes first or what causes what; whether low self-image leads one to become anorexic or if having the eating disorder upsets one's sense of self. It is clear that the eating disorder is intricately tied up with self-esteem.

Toward the end of our hour, Janine also told us that she'd been 100 percent that whole day, meaning she'd eaten all her meals and all her snacks with no stand-in Ensure.

"I just decided to do it," she explained breezily. "I just set a goal."

I wondered if it was significant that she set this goal on the very day she'd be seeing us for therapy. Did she want us to be proud of her? Did she want to make sure that her passes home weren't jeopardized again? She had once told me that being on med protocol was comforting. Same with her meal plan. It was reassuring to have someone else be in charge of your calories in and calories out. Did she realize now that hanging around the dorm on med protocol was not so comforting after all? That, even though it might provoke some anxiety at first, perhaps taking a chance on us as foster parents might, in the end, provide more lasting comfort? We could only hope.

And with that hope came love.

I remember distinctly the exact moment when I realized that I really did love Janine. We were planning to take her home on another pass. Then Ben called. Her weight had dropped. She was once again on med protocol. We couldn't take her home with us after all. I sat down, the phone still in my hand. I felt heavy. I couldn't speak. I was disappointed, yes. But what I was feeling was more than just an adjustment to an unexpected change of plans. I was devastated. My throat closed. My nose itched. I realized I was going to cry. That's when I knew: I loved her.

We fall in love with our children at different moments and in different ways. The first fetal flip. The grainy ultrasound image. The metronome heartbeat. Sometimes we fall in love with them when they are just an idea, a plan, a goal. Trying to get pregnant. Going through the adoption process. Whatever it is. Our children prick our hearts long before they mean to. Sometimes before they even exist. Certainly, before we become a family. Maybe only a blueprint. We were only just getting to know Janine. We were not even officially her foster parents yet. That would not happen until she actually came home to live with us, an event that was still nine months away.

Love doesn't always follow a prescribed timeline. Sometimes love just is. What was this love I felt for Janine? Where had it come from? This aching? This stir? She had certainly stood out in my practice, as much for her brains and beauty as for her mother's unpredictability and histrionics. She didn't deserve to lose her father so young. To have a mother whose struggles with alcohol and mental illness made caring for her daughters impossible. Abandoned and estranged, it was no small wonder that she had shrunk her world to one manageable bite—literally—and become an anorexic.

When does admiration or fondness turn into love? It wasn't love we felt when Janine's CASA worker told us she was coming up on a year in Clinton Care, no motivation to conquer her eating disorder because she had nowhere to go after discharge. It wasn't love that prompted us to step forward and offer to become her foster parents. Altruism, maybe. Or wanting to give back. We raised two healthy boys who had flown our nest and become confident, independent adults. We still had some love, some parenting left to give. And when we met her—all koala-slippered and chattering about music and animals—that wasn't love either. Maybe wonder for all she had been through and excitement for all she could become. Heartbreak, maybe, that this little egg of potential was not hatching. But not love.

When I was a young woman, I equated love with a feeling. Those gooey, heart-flipping moments when we think of our beloved. But as

I've gotten older, I've come to understand love in a different way. Yes, it's still about feelings (and those feelings were with me on the phone with Ben that day with my melting heart, swollen eyes and dripping nose). Love to me now was more about commitment and loyalty. A resolution to stick by someone no matter what muddies the waters.

There is no obligation to love in foster care. There is no expectation that a foster parent will fall in love with the child the state gives us—temporarily. There may even be a guarding against love, knowing that the department can remove this child at any moment from our care. In all our discussions with DCF about volunteering to be the girls' foster parents, the word love was never mentioned. In the handbook that would be given to us—in a stark office with a two-way mirror and child-sized table and chairs, where we would be fingerprinted and notarized, and sign on the dotted line—it never came up. There were rules we had to follow, promises we needed make: to take them regularly to the doctor and dentist, to use the quarterly-allocated clothing check only for clothing. We had to agree to follow whatever plan DCF deemed was in the child's best interest whether we agreed with it or not. There was no recommendation for love. And yet there I was. A melted, sniveling mess, and definitely in love.

"We think about Janine all the time," Saul mused after our next therapy session with Janine and Ben. "Do you think she ever thinks about us?"

I had no answer to his query. It just touched me to my core that he even asked the question.

———

For our next pass, we decided to take Janine to the Franklin Park Zoo. She loved animals and the zoo was close by.

When we arrived, Sara opened the door, saying, "C'mon in. I'll go get Janine." It was strangely thrilling for me to be recognized and associated with our foster daughter. It also meant that she was not on med protocol.

Once again, Janine came down dressed in thin layers: a long-sleeved jersey over a tee with a wound-around infinity scarf, jeans and Sperrys.

"Do you even own a winter coat?" Saul asked.

"Yup," Janine replied, suddenly grinning. "Wanna know why I didn't wear it?"

"Sure."

She stuck out a tan shoe and fingered her brown and orange print scarf and said, "Because it doesn't match my outfit."

Saul just shook his head and smiled.

"Go get your coat."

The zoo was in winter mode already. Visitors were scarce and not all the exhibits were open. As we walked, we kept hearing the deep rumbling roar of a lion. We would run over to his cage every time, only to find him sitting in regal silence. We began to wonder if the roar was just piped in sound effects. At one point, when we ran back hoping to catch the animal mid-roar only to find him lumbering towards some shade, we asked a father and son at the exhibit, "Did that lion just roar?" They nodded and left. Determined, we camped out at the exhibit. Suddenly a jet plane thundered overhead. The lion lifted his head and roared as if in response. We skipped away, singing Katy Perry's "Roar" at the tops of our lungs.

We finished our zoo trip over the next couple of hours, strolling through the exhibits of white tigers, zebras, gorillas, wattled cranes, flamingoes and wildebeests. As we were walking toward the exit, Janine noticed painted animal prints on the sidewalks. Saul guessed they were zebra tracks as we had come in the zebra entrance. Janine wondered aloud if they were real.

"Do you think they dip the zebra's hooves in paint and lead him along the sidewalk?"

"I don't think so," Saul answered. "It's not bug art."

Janine and I cracked up. And there it was: our first inside joke. Bug art. Something that only we three would find funny. We three who had been to the bug art exhibit at the Peabody Essex Museum and seen the zebra prints at the Franklin Park Zoo. Something no one else in the world had experienced or would get.

It wouldn't be the first time we shared an inside joke, just the three of us. One afternoon we were playing Scrabble in the conference room at Clinton Care when Janine was on med protocol. When Saul stood up to go to the bathroom, he disrupted some of the letters on the board. As we straightened them out, Janine noticed that two separate words, "berry" and "shad," had gotten smushed together as one word. She made a pouty, frowny face.

"That's berry shad," she joked.

A couple of weeks later, we went to visit Janine only to be told by staff that she was feeling so depressed that she didn't even want to come out of her room to see us. I wanted to respect her decision, not force a visit on her if she truly didn't want it. On the other hand, she had told us that weekends with no visitors could be very long at Clinton Care. I didn't want her to have any regrets.

"Tell her we respect her decision," I told staff. "Tell her we'll leave if she wants us to. But tell her that would make us berry shad."

Sara looked a bit puzzled but took the message up to Janine. After a few minutes, sure enough, Janine poked her head into the conference room.

"Well, I didn't want you to be berry shad," she said. A second inside joke. Saving our visit from cancellation. More important, making us feel like we were becoming a family.

FOUR

A Relationship
in Venn Diagrams

I was beginning to feel the strain of the eating disorder and fostering. It had only been a few months since we'd been working with Janine, but I was discouraged with her slow progress and how little it took to make her anxious. She was discouraged, too, I know.

"I've been on med protocol *sooo* many times," she complained to me one day on the phone as we were discussing Thanksgiving, which was just a few weeks away. At this point we were calling Janine in her dorm room or she was calling us several times a week.

"I know, but you've also gone your longest stretch *off* med protocol *ever*," I countered.

"I *hate* med protocol! You can't *do* anything on med protocol!" she wailed.

"Good!" I exclaimed. "Because you used to *like* being on med protocol. You found it comforting. This is *progress*," I assured her.

At the end of the conversation, I said, "I love you."

"I love you too," she replied. I hadn't meant to say it. It just came out. I had been thinking a lot about love lately—ever since I cried when I learned I couldn't see Janine. Ever since I knew I was in love. I hadn't intended to burden her. It was just an honest declaration.

I was chastised for it by Ben. He didn't even wait for our next therapy session, calling me on the phone instead. He called it anxiety-provoking. (I was beginning to wonder what *wasn't* anxiety-provoking.) He acknowledged how emotionally intense this whole process was for us. Again, he encouraged us, me, to slow down.

It made me feel like a failure and I sobbed uncontrollably after that

31

call. I felt so stupid. I hadn't meant to do damage. I wasn't intentionally trying to pull Janine toward us or rush the relationship along. I was just being truthful. Just telling her how I felt. It wasn't planned. It just popped out. I didn't expect anything in return.

In our next therapy session, I addressed my faux pas head-on with Janine.

"Look," I told her frankly. "I will always make mistakes. I cannot promise you that I will always know the right thing to say. But I can promise you this. I will always try. I can learn from my mistakes. And the more you're willing to tell me what I'm doing wrong, the better I'll get at being supportive."

We talked about her people-pleasing and how it would be more helpful to me and Saul if she'd tell us if she were anxious or sad or depressed. She didn't have to hide behind a smile. In fact, that had to be exhausting for her.

"That would be rude," she protested.

"Why?" I asked.

"Because that would be dumping myself on you and asking you to fix me."

It made me feel like we were living in two different worlds. In our world, we look at her and she's smiling and chatty and we think everything's fine. In her world, inside her, it's different. It's scary or anxious or dark and we don't even know and that made me sad.

Suddenly, I had an idea.

"Do you know what a Venn diagram is?" I asked her. She tipped her head to one side, not answering. I asked Ben for a piece of paper and drew two side-by-side circles with a tiny sliver of overlap.

"Here's your world," I said shading one of the circles in gray.

"And here's our world." I pointed to the uncolored circle. Then I lightly cross-hatched the ellipse-shaped common area.

"And this is where we meet and where our worlds are the same." I drew two more circles with a much bigger area of overlap.

"And the more you let us into your world," I explained, "the more our worlds will be the same."

She pondered the circles with that same cocked-head look and furrowed brow, nodding. I think she got it.

In another session, Saul asked her if it would be wrong to ask if she wanted mayonnaise on her sandwich.

"Not wrong, exactly," she answered. "Just not helpful."

Ben re-iterated to Saul a point he'd made before, that eating disorder wasn't about taste. Saul still couldn't fathom this. In his mind, it had to be easier to eat something—even if you forced yourself to eat it—if it tasted good. So he persisted.

"But would it be wrong to put mayonnaise on your..."

"Yes!" Janine cut him off loudly and abruptly. We all looked at her.

"Well, that felt good," she said quietly with a sheepish smile.

"I agree," Saul added, nodding emphatically.

It was a small thing, but it let Janine know she could say things to us and we wouldn't break. More important, we wouldn't leave.

———

As Thanksgiving got closer, Janine's anxiety level increased. We asked her what she'd done last Thanksgiving. She told us she had gone to her Nana's house. Initially she waxed nostalgic about how her mom was there and Mariah and all her cousins and how much fun they'd had. Eventually, though, she admitted that she had found the whole thing so overwhelming that she'd spent the entire day crying in the upstairs bathroom.

Saul made it clear to Janine (and to Ben) that she was welcome at our home for Thanksgiving. He wanted her to know she had a place to go—where she would be with people who understood her eating disorder and could coach her through a meal. Janine insisted she'd be fine going to her Nana's. Ben finally intervened.

"Everything about your behavior is telling me you're stressing out about this. I'm taking it out of your hands. You're not going anywhere. Not your Nana's. Not the Bornsteins' either."

Janine protested mildly but I could see she was relieved to have this decided for her. I had to admit Ben probably made the right call. I did worry that it wasn't teaching Janine the skill of saying no, the art of self-care. But there was no denying the relief in Janine's face when she was told she'd be spending Thanksgiving at the program.

Section I—In the Beginning

The truth was that, on some level, I was relieved too. I loved Janine and would have welcomed her to our table with widespread arms. But that table would be crowded and loud and messy, not to mention piled high with a million courses. None of our family had met Janine yet. Someone was bound to say something triggering. How would I divide myself? How would I catch up with my grown sons while protecting my fragile girl from a misplaced word?

On Thanksgiving Day, as I mashed potatoes and baked bread and salted soup and tossed salad, I thought about Janine. If she were here, she would probably be up in her room trying to ignore the sounds and smells of the holiday. Saul would probably take her with him on his daily walk with Homer at Mosley Pines. I'd probably be stressed, needing him to drag up tables and chairs from the cellar but not wanting him to have to leave Janine alone with her thoughts. Would she have spent the whole day crying in our bathroom, too? Or would she have made small talk with a table full of still-strangers-not-yet-family?

People arrived bearing armloads of pies and sides.

"How's Janine?" each asked, either by way of greeting at the door or over coffee after the meal. I answered each question as best I could. Food would stress her. She's at the program. No, she didn't go to her family either. Behind the questions was a deep concern for this child they had not yet met. And underneath my answers was a sadness at that fact. I missed her, her absence hollow at the table. A weighty want in my heart.

<hr />

On our next visit with Janine, we walked into the conference room of Clinton Care only to find her sprawled face down across the table, arms wrapped around her head, a glass of Ensure untouched in front of her. A staff member sat beside her, her hands in her lap. She gave us a silent little wave and motioned for us to sit down, too. We took seats across from Janine and tried unsuccessfully to engage her in conversation.

After a few minutes, the staff member looked at her watch, then took the undrunk supplement and left the room. Saul pulled a chair up next to Janine and said, "Having a tough time of it, huh?" She rolled her head to one side to face him, her hair still masking her face.

"Yup, I'm definitely on the struggle bus today," she said and promptly turned her face back down toward the table. Saul reached up and patted her shoulder, then rubbed her back in small circles. He kept talking to her.

"What's wrong? How can we help?"

I knew his well-intentioned touch—meant only to comfort—was somehow wrong. I shook my head at him, slashed my finger across my throat to signal "cut it out" and mouthed "no." At first, he just scowled at me in a "I know what I'm doing" kind of way. Eventually he stopped. Janine took a few more minutes in her silent cocoon and then joined us in conversation.

The rest of the visit went pretty well. We had bought her a new game called the Settlers of Catan and had fun learning how to play it. I had bought her a pair of Christmas socks, which she loved.

At our next therapy session, we sat with Ben in his office alone as we normally did. This time he started off with a grave "Janine won't be joining us today." Saul looked momentarily confused. I knew exactly what was coming. An admonishment over touch.

We knew Janine had a history of sexual abuse by a family friend when she was younger. I knew as Janine's pediatrician. Now, Ben was describing Janine's trauma history to Saul and telling us that because of it, she just didn't know how to interpret touch. He tried to assure Saul that he knew his intentions were good. His heart was in the right place. He was just following his instincts. Comforting Janine in the same way he would his own sons. But being abused at such a young age had left Janine misunderstanding even paternal touch.

"Think of Janine as having a giant gaping wound in her side," Ben told Saul. "You wouldn't just walk up and hug someone with a gaping wound, would you?"

I knew what he was getting at, but I thought it was a poor analogy. All I could think was *Well, no, but isn't the person with the gaping wound the one who needs hugging the most?* It was understandable what he was saying. But I worried it would leave Saul with the same shamed and miserable feeling I'd had when I'd been chastened by Ben for blurting out *I love you* too soon.

The only crumb of comfort I felt was when Ben acknowledged how difficult this all was for us. Because how to respond to Janine went against every instinct we had as parents or even as human beings.

"You want to comfort her. To show her you care," Ben acknowledged. We nodded. "But that's not what Janine needs. What she needs is structure and routine. That's what will comfort her. That's how she'll feel safe."

I asked Ben if he just validated Janine's feelings (*Yeah, it must be scary to be touched by an older man*) or if he tried to explain to her that Saul was just being paternal. Just trying to make her feel better.

"Both!" he said.

I must have looked disappointed. It wasn't the answer I was looking for.

"Believe me, Carolyn, I'm constantly urging Janine toward you guys. I tell her all the time what a gift you are in her life." He went on to say that she knows she's headed toward us as a foster placement. He made it sound as if we were an inevitable car crash.

I sat through the entire session blinking back tears. I let them fall the minute I was out the door. Saul reached across the front seat of the car and stroked my hair.

"Don't let him get to you, Cal," he said. "Every kid needs touch; I don't care what Ben says." Saul and I reacted so differently to criticism. He had an unshakeable confidence, even if he wasn't the expert in the field. A water-off-a-duck's-back approach to life. Me? I tended to carry others' words in me like rocks in a gizzard. I churned them constantly, worrying them smooth.

Tears streamed down my face and my shoulders shook with silent sobs. I wondered if Ben had any idea how badly he made me feel. Like we were both failed parents in his eyes. Like we made everything worse. Saul with his touch, me with my words.

Even as Ben had told us in our session how pleased he was with how things were going, that the degree of comfort Janine felt with us and the positive way she spoke about us was so much more secure and attached than it had been at the beginning of September, I had still felt like he was just throwing us bones. I still felt judged for how we handled situations on our own. He told us that things were going to just move incrementally forward with lots of bumps along the way. The implication seemed to be that all of the bumps were our doing. And he had left us with his favorite warning.

"Slow down."

FIVE

Facing Demons

Saul and I, being Jewish, had never had a Christmas tree in our whole married life. But we were determined to make our home welcoming to Janine for the holiday season. We bought a tree and I put out a plea to my friends asking for any decorations they didn't use anymore. I'd even come pick them up. The response was overwhelming. Bags and boxes of tinsel, stars and angels poured in. Some people sent ornaments that must have been in their families forever: painted glass orbs and delicate reindeer. Others went out and bought brand new decorations for this girl they'd never met.

Janine spent an entire Saturday home pass carefully creating a masterpiece of the tree with her artistic eye and streak of perfectionism. She carefully wound strands of tiny white lights around the tree, standing back to assess her placement, then correcting: one branch up, half an inch in. Next went the ornaments: plastic candy canes, glittering stars, fat Santas. When she had finished, we had a six-foot work of art in our living room.

We surprised Janine the next day with front row seats to a production of *The Nutcracker* in Boston. Our friend Joe had been playing Mother Ginger in the show ever since his daughter Olivia was a ballet dancer with the troupe. Olivia was now a 25-year-old journalist, but Joe was still Mother Ginger. When the curtains went up, Janine let out a small gasp. The dancers' white tutus gleamed blue in the soft stage lighting. Falling snow landed on our laps, and when fog rolled in at the beginning of the second act, it blew cold in our faces.

The story played out. Clara receiving the nutcracker as a present. The mean boys stealing it from her, teasing her with it and then breaking it. The nutcracker turning into a real prince. Dolls coming to life. Finally, Joe came out as Mother Ginger on stilts with a wide skirt hiding 12 children (or as Joe liked to put it, "24 little feet I have to try not to step on").

After the play, Joe took Janine backstage. He showed her the fog machine and how they made snow fall. His stilts. The toy soldier costumes. We took photos with our phones, Janine's smile wider in each frame.

Through the whole holiday season, though, something was missing: Janine's sister Mariah. After coming forward to be both girls' foster parents, we didn't hear one word about Mariah from DCF. She may have finally unpacked her bags at her new foster home. If she did, we were never told. We had prepared our guest room for a teenage girl whom we thought would be Mariah. Instead, we'd shown it to Janine as hers. Since the girls' social worker Syd Reynolds told us, "Forget about Mariah. Concentrate on Janine," they had never updated us once on her situation.

Until...

Out of the blue, on a Tuesday in mid–January, DCF called me at work asking if I would take Mariah "as an emergency placement."

"Of course we'll take her," I told the worker. "Bring her by my office at five."

Mariah showed up at the appointed hour. All of her belongings were stuffed in the back of her social worker's car. We transferred them from her trunk to mine in the dark of the parking lot. Plastic hampers full of clothes. A green and blue plaid backpack. A white pocketbook with school texts and notebooks spilling out. Two black trash bags filled with who knew what. As Mariah loaded a cardboard box into my back seat, a Hillsboro Bank checkbook slid to the asphalt.

This was no way to live.

As I was helping Mariah transfer her belongings, she told me she had recently gotten her learner's permit. When it was time to leave, I dropped my keys into the palm of her hand.

"Really?" she asked, incredulous. "You're letting me drive home?"

"Of course," I answered nonchalantly, trying not to show my delight at her use of the word "home."

Section I—In the Beginning

She was taking her road test in two days. My office was an easy backroads 10-mile drive. I knew she would do fine. I also thought it would show her that I trusted her. Had confidence in her. Believed in her.

On the way home, she told me how unfairly she felt she'd been treated by Elaine, her last foster mom. She thought Elaine put on one face for DCF, then turned into an entirely different person behind closed doors. She was in her 50s with no children of her own.

"You shouldn't even be allowed to be a foster parent if you don't have kids," Mariah muttered. There was another teenage girl in the house who was a homebody which made the contrast with Mariah's gregarious nature stark.

"I just want to be out with my friends," she complained. From what I gathered from my conversation with DCF, Mariah, despite a 9 o'clock weekday and 11 o'clock weekend curfew, was rarely home. Things had come to a head two nights before when Elaine called the cops on Mariah, reporting her as a runaway. They had put Mariah in a temporary emergency foster home the night before. There was an 18-year-old boy there who made Mariah very uncomfortable.

"I've had some not-so-nice things happen to me in some of my foster homes," she told me by way of explanation. She'd refused to return for a second night. That's when DCF called me.

"I don't deserve this," she steamed, eyes on the road.

Indeed, she did not. She didn't deserve a dead father or an alcoholic mother or whatever abuse she'd suffered in the past. She didn't deserve 11 foster homes in five years.

We stopped at the grocery store on the way home. I told her to pick out whatever she liked. She liked chicken parm and mozzarella and tomato salad and bags of Pirate Booty. She told me she made a mean guacamole. I told her I did, too.

"Sounds like a guac-off," she quipped, throwing avocadoes and limes into the cart.

"Hey, can I apply for a job while we're here?" she suddenly asked.

Oh, my girl. What love and admiration I felt for her in that moment. Her birthday was tomorrow. She would turn seventeen. The day after that she would take her driver's license test. She had just been moved from one foster home to another on an emergency basis. And here she was, wanting to work, too. God bless her.

"Of course," I said.

The next day was the anniversary of their father's death. I had Mariah dismissed early. We were meeting Janine and Ben at the cemetery. Mariah knew right where her father's gravestone was. She opted to wait in the car until Janine got there. I walked up to Jimmy's grave and placed a handful of found rocks on top, a Jewish tradition. A Boston Bruins emblem was embedded in the front of the marker. Two built-in vases on either side held faded plastic flowers. I brought my index finger to my lips, then pushed the kiss into the top of the gravestone.

"I'm trying, Jimmy," I whispered. "I'll take care of them for you. I'll do my best."

Ben finally pulled up with Janine who carried a plastic-wrapped bouquet of bright orange dahlias. The girls tossed the old plastic bouquets into my trunk and replaced them with fresh flowers. Janine arranged and rearranged—a blossom here, a green there—reminding me of how she had so carefully decorated our Christmas tree.

The girls shivered in their thin sweaters and hoodies. They knelt side by side, their knees in soggy puddles of old snow. Ben and I hung back, giving them their time and space.

I thought about Jimmy. How proud he would be of his girls. How glad he would be that they would finally be under the same roof again. I remembered watching him fade as the cancer overtook him, balding as the chemo failed to stop it. I had tried desperately to get him into hospice care. I had called my friend Jen Reilly who was the director of the program. There was nothing she could do. The order had to come from Jimmy's oncologist who had stubbornly refused.

"He's hospice-averse," Jen had explained grimly. "He thinks he can save all his patients."

Jimmy died on a ventilator. No cancer patient should have to die like that. I felt I had failed him. Maybe I was trying to make up for it now by taking care of his children as best I could. To apologize to him for not doing enough.

The girls rose slowly from their knees, ready to go home. Ben handed me a Ziploc bag with Janine's dinner: two veggie burgers, pita bread, salad, sliced almonds, and milk. He told me she'd made her weight by just a couple of ounces. We drove off, the girls playing the radio, singing softly along.

I asked if we could stop at Market Basket on the way home. Janine said, "Okay" in a way that let me know that it wasn't. So I just had Mariah drop off her job application and we drove home. Janine sat at the counter in the kitchen. Saul had bought Mariah a bouquet of flowers her first night home with a card that read, "Welcome to our home." She had told us that night, "This doesn't feel like a foster home. It just feels like home."

I ran out to Market Basket by myself after settling the girls in to watch TV. I bought identical foods to Janine's: veggie burgers, pita bread, salad. She had told us that it helped her with her meal if we were all eating the same thing. When I walked in the door, Janine announced brightly, "They plated my meal wrong. I'm only supposed to have one veggie burger for dinner. I just talked to Corey. You can call him back if you want."

We signed papers every time we took Janine on a pass, assuring that we would be with her at all times. I had left her alone, thinking she was at home, safe with her sister. Now she had schemed her way out of a veggie burger. I knew she hadn't called Corey. I couldn't call him either without exposing myself as a breaker of rules, an abandoner, and she knew it. There went 100 calories down the drain.

She ate her meal slowly, taking her burger out of the pita, picking pieces off it, putting it back. Not so long ago, she had proudly announced, "Guess what I did today."

"What?"

"Ate a sandwich the normal way!" Now she was deconstructing it and reassembling it again like she had that very first meal at our house four months earlier. Was she regressing? Or was this just a manifestation of grief?

As we all chatted over our empty plates after finishing our meals, Janine crunched loudly on her ice. I'd forgotten to pour her milk. I'd poured her ice water, same as the rest of us.

"Oh, Janine, I'm sorry," I said, realizing my mistake too late. "Let me get your milk." She hurriedly dropped her empty plate in the sink, ran into the living room and plopped down on the couch. I brought her the carton of milk staff had packed for her. She ignored me.

"You can take it with you in the car," I suggested, the hour she would have to leave to go back to the program fast approaching. She shook her head.

"I'll pour it in a glass for you," I offered, pulling the tiny plastic straw from the carton. I stopped pleading when I saw a single tear escape down her cheek. Curled up, unable to even speak. Then I knew. It must be another of her rigid rules. Once she'd left the table, she was done. There was no going back.

When it was time to leave, I gave Janine a sideways hug like they do in the program. There were no frontal hugs allowed between residents and with staff. Mariah gave her sister a full-on hug which both girls seemed reluctant to end. Watching Janine climb into Saul's car for the long ride back to the program, I was glad for Mariah's company. Excited for us to be creeping toward the time we would be a real family.

<hr>

In mid–February, Janine came off her meal plan. While part of her wanted to take this step, it was nevertheless very stressful. One of the problems with disordered eating is disordered perception. She sees obesity in the mirror even though she weighs 90 pounds. Similarly, a normal half-cup serving of rice, to Janine, could look like a mound on her plate the size of a volleyball. When she was on her meal plan, she constantly had me re-measuring her portions. Eight ounces of milk looked like 8.1 to her and she would stand at the kitchen sink drip drip dripping milk drop by drop down the drain until she was satisfied it was back to precisely eight.

"Your perception is distorted by your disease," I once told her, spooning the half cup of rice back into the measuring cup to prove I'd plated the correct amount.

"If my perception is so distorted, why don't you just gouge my eyes out?!" she'd yelled.

The staff at Clinton Care had pushed her off meal plan faster than was the original goal. Initially she was supposed to first plate only her breakfast. If that went well, then after a while she would plate lunch, too, and so on. But somewhere along the line, someone on staff decided that if she could do breakfast, she could do everything else. Then boom. She was on her own.

She would call us from the program in tears.

"My stomach hurts! I'm so fat!" she'd wail.

Still, she was 100 percent, completing every meal and all her snacks with no Ensure replacements. I tried to be sympathetic to her utter angst being off meal plan and at the same time encouraging that this was a huge and necessary step in her recovery.

Toward the end of one particular conversation, a staff member started trying to get Janine to hang up the phone. It was time for hygiene.

"I'm talking to my foster parents. *They're* helping me!" she shrieked at the staff member. "*You're* not helping me!"

It broke our hearts to have to hang up. We told her we loved her. "Love you, too," she parroted. Five months ago, that was such a loaded phrase for her. Now there was an urgency to it. A necessity. It was an integral part of our conversations. We love you. It is important for you to know this. It is part of your treatment to be loved.

Her first weekend home on pass being off meal plan was taxing. I had come to realize that the only reason Janine even ate when she was home was that she trusted the program not to make her fat. If she just ate the food they packed for her, she knew she would stay within her narrow weight range. Now she was being asked to trust us, too.

I needn't have worried. I made chicken salad sandwiches with fruit and milk for lunch. She ate every bite. We had fried fish for dinner with a side dish made with faro, spinach and pine nuts. Janine practically inhaled it.

"What kind of fish is this?"

"Haddock."

"Mmm. I haven't had this in so long. What kind of grain is this?"

"Faro."

"I've never even heard of faro."

I was used to eating slowly when I ate with Janine in an effort to match her pace. She liked to be the last one done. She felt that if she finished first, it meant that she ate too fast. It would mean she was a glutton, her eating disorder shaming her inside her head. This night, when I looked over at Janine's plate, she was almost done. I had to hurry to keep up with her. Maybe the one who felt safe being on a meal plan was her eating disorder. Maybe the starving girl inside of her illness felt deprived. And that girl was starting to enjoy eating again.

I read Harriet Brown's memoir *Brave Girl Eating* at Janine's recommendation. It details her daughter's struggle with an eating disorder. In the first scene, she asks the reader to imagine being at a bakery, nose pressed against glass. Looking at the flaky puff pastries, creamy éclairs and sticky Napoleons. Smelling loaves of bread baking in brick ovens. Feeling the warmth as the oven door opens. Imagine all that. Then imagine not being allowed to eat even a single nibble. That's what living with an eating disorder was like, Brown told us. I read the book when I had just begun working with Janine—watching her quake at the thought of food, hiding almonds in her sleeves and stuffing them down the drain later to avoid eating them. I thought Brown had it all wrong. People with anorexia are repulsed by food. Food is the enemy.

"No!" Janine corrected me one day. "That's *exactly* what it's like."

Now, watching Janine enjoy a healthy meal of fish and faro, I finally understood. That small sad girl inside of anorexia *was* hungry. She *did* have her nose pressed against the bakery glass. It was the eating disorder itself telling her she couldn't have it. She's too fat already. She doesn't deserve it.

Here was our own brave girl starting to claw her way out of her illness. Like a character at Disney World with a fuzzy blue costume, a giant fake head with mesh over the eyes. You could peer in and see there was a human being in there. It felt like Janine was just beginning to emerge. To lift off that fuzzy blue head and say, "It's me! I'm here and I love faro!"

Section I—In the Beginning

It was a fine balance between healthy activity and obsession. Between inspiration and trigger. At Clinton Care when she was not on med protocol, she could do an "active activity" once or twice a day. It might be going to the workout room or taking a walk or simply going on a field trip to Walgreen's for hygiene products with the other girls. If she was on med protocol, all of that was out.

So when she and Mariah wanted to sign up for the gym together, I thought it might be a good idea. We'd gone sledding and roller-skating and bowling on her February school vacation and she'd made her goal weight at check-in mid-week. Surely she could tolerate a little exercise and not lose weight. Besides, it would give the girls some much needed "sister time," as they called it.

One morning, after we had all three spent an hour at the gym, I fixed lunch, then called the girls. Only Mariah came down. I went upstairs and found Janine rocking back and forth on her bed, clutching her stuffed animal Woolfie to her chest. Her stare was trance-like.

"What's wrong?" I gulped, climbing onto the bed beside her.

"I. Don't. Want. To. Eat." Her words came out with great effort. Her voice was gravelly. It looked like it was hard for her to breathe. My heart dropped. I knew she didn't just mean "I'm not hungry right now." I knew she meant she didn't want to eat. As in ever again. I knew I was staring eating disorder right in the face. It was inhabiting her, like an un-exorcised demon, right before my eyes.

"What happened?" I asked. An hour ago, we'd been cooling down together on the ab mats next to the track, chit-chatting. Now this.

"Body image issues," she managed. Her words slurred, like it was hard for her just to move her mouth. She continued to rock, her body curled around Woolfie. I was truly unnerved by what I was seeing. I tried to help her, like they do at the program. Identify what it was that triggered this response.

"Did you see something at the gym?" I prompted. She nodded.

"There were people who looked..." She hesitated, struggling with the effort of speech. I tried to fill in.

"What? Skinny? Pretty?" She shook her head.

"Like death."

I sat back, confused. I had seen no one there that looked like death. Everyone was either healthy and fit or trying to be. I thought about a woman I used to see at the gym who was clearly anorexic. She'd swim for hours, then teeter back to the locker room on legs thin as twine. I wondered how the gym could let her exercise constantly like that when she so clearly needed help. I hadn't seen her in years.

"I only saw healthy people there," I told Janine honestly.

"I have an eating disorder," she explained. "I seek them out. Then I fixate on them."

She seemed to be getting her voice back. Coming out of her trance. Whatever was possessing her was losing its grip. She seemed to be slogging her way back from wherever she'd been. Where would she go if I let her? Where would she be if I hadn't come upstairs?

I told her we could wait a while before eating. The girls had been planning to visit their cousin Amy. Clearly Janine wasn't going anywhere.

"You're not going to Amy's," I told her, taking the decision out of her hands like Ben had had to do so many times before. I didn't expect any resistance and I got none. "Saul will drive Mariah there in about an hour, and while they're gone, you and I will go downstairs and eat. Then maybe we'll go to the beach. The fresh air will do you good."

She set Woolfie down against her pillow and shook her head, slowly coming back into herself. Shaking off the clutch of eating disorder.

"No," she said. "Let's eat now. If I wait, I'll just obsess and decide to refuse."

I followed her down the stairs and into the kitchen thinking this is what courage looks like. Powering through. This is strong. This is brave.

―――∞∞∞―――

That spring, I gave a keynote address to the Brain Injury Association of Rhode Island. Ever since I had written *Crash,* I was regularly invited to speak at various conferences and symposia. It always left me inspired, not just sharing my story, but also hearing from others. It also helped me to feel more dimensional than I usually did these days. So often I felt like my only role, the one that took front and center in my life every day, was being a foster mom, often a bad one at that. So it felt good to be seen as a professional: a doctor, a speaker, an expert.

I was taken to lunch by one of the board members of the BIA who herself had a child with a traumatic brain injury. Although we technically shared the same experience—our children had both been hit by drunk drivers—her daughter's injuries were worse than my son's. She was in a wheelchair and unable to communicate. One of the lectures at the conference had been a demonstration of a new technology that allowed TBI survivors to communicate through the blink of an eye or even a glance in a certain direction. I asked my host about it; she told me that she had taken her daughter to communication experts all over the country only to be given no hope.

"There's nothing there," she said flatly.

I admired her tremendously in that moment—giving unilaterally to her child who could not intentionally give back. Most of us love our children unconditionally, without any expectation of anything in return. When our babies look at us for the first time, smile their first smile, say "Mama," those are bonuses. We would love them anyway. It doesn't change our love. That's a constant. A given. But those moments certainly do help to fill the well. A tiny gift that makes it all worth it, even when the road gets cluttered with obstacles.

I was so grateful for what I had. With all our struggles with the girls, there were so many moments of pleasure and pride. Moments that filled the well. Watching Mariah give it her all at the gym. Applying for a job the very day she was placed with us. Being praised by her boss for her work ethic. Even once when Mariah got suspended from school, I admired her toughness. Another girl had been following her around her classes for days harassing her. Mariah kept her nose down and her mouth shut, trying to mind her own business and just do her work. But when the girl sat behind Mariah and pulled her hair, that was the end of her patience. She punched her in the face. It wasn't exactly how I would have handled things. Then again, I hadn't been through what Mariah had in her young life. I had parents to stand up for me. Mariah had had to stand up for herself. She was a survivor.

I admired Janine, too. The courage she showed facing down her inner demons was an inspiration. The fortitude it took for tiny acts—sipping a drink or forking a noodle—showed in her furrowed brow, her shaking leg, sometimes in the tears that streamed down her face.

Since Janine had lost two pounds on her last weigh-in, she was no longer on "snacks optional" and evening snack was the hardest for her. After thinking about all the calories she had consumed during the day—breakfast, snack, lunch, snack, dinner—it was almost too much to bear to think about putting even one more morsel into her mouth. The night I came home after keynoting, I made her a smoothie for evening snack naively thinking that maybe it would be easier for her to drink her snack than to eat it. Janine heard the blender whirring and raced upstairs. I followed her with her smoothie. Saul beat me to her. She was sprawled out on her bed, miserable at the thought of having to consume calories. Again. It saddened me to see her struggle with something so mundane. So necessary. Feeding her body.

Someone once told me that treating eating disorder was more difficult than treating alcoholism or heroin addiction. With those ailments, they said, you had to lock the lion in its cage and throw away the key. With eating disorder, you had to free the lion three times a day for meals, three times a day for snacks, play with it, then wrestle the beast back into its cage each time. As I watched Janine fight every bite, the analogy felt apt.

When it was clear that all my cajoling and coaxing was not moving Janine any closer to starting her snack, Saul finally hoisted her up over his shoulder and carried her downstairs. At first, he huffed and puffed and groaned. I motioned frantically for him to stop, fearing that Janine would wail, "I'm so fat, you can't even carry me," and any hope of getting snack into her would evaporate.

As sometimes happens with our children, she surprised us. I often tell parents of toddlers in my practice who are afraid to get rid of the pacifier, for example, afraid their child will wail and moan

and be generally inconsolable without it, "They might surprise you."
I think sometimes we fear the worst. But maybe we need to have a
little faith. Believe in our kids. They're stronger than we think sometimes.

And Janine was strong tonight. She sat right down at the kitchen
table and drank her smoothie. Every bit. She even tipped the plastic
glass up, catching the last few drops with her tongue. I didn't know
what it was. Maybe sheer resolve. Or maybe the starving girl inside
the monster of eating disorder was saying, "Hey, I'm hungry." Whatever it was, I'd take it. I did a little victory dance inside my head.

Oh my girl.

My lion-tamer.

Six

It Takes Courage to Believe

During one of our last therapy sessions before Janine was discharged from Clinton Care, we walked into Ben's office to find a huge poster taped to one of his walls. At the top of the sheet, he had written in Magic Marker the words "Obstacles I Have Overcome." He handed Janine a stack of colored construction paper and the marker. While Saul and I watched, she wrote down all the challenges, traumas and obstacles that she had surmounted in her young life. Then she taped each piece of paper onto the blank poster board.

It filled up quickly.

Some of the losses were huge and devastating. No child should have to endure them. "My father's death" filled the first sheet. "My mother's alcoholism" the second. Those were major losses: ongoing sorrows to be dealt with in therapy.

Then she added some obstacles we were already helping her to address. "Living without my sister" on pink paper. "Living without my cats" on black. Mariah was now our foster daughter. We adopted the girls' cats from an animal shelter when her mom grew too sick to care for them. We could help lighten that burden. Restore something lost.

Other quotes evoked a more specific fear. "Being afraid someone I live with will hurt me" she wrote on green paper and "Living with people who were not nice to me" on orange.

I had to ask Janine for clarification of one of the quotes. On purple paper, she had written, "Being afraid of making a mistake."

"What does that mean?" I asked quietly.

"In foster care, you always feel like if you do something wrong, you can be taken away and sent somewhere else." My heart cracked. She then made a point of saying, "Oh, I don't feel that way with you guys." She frowned and waved her hands in the air as if to physically dissipate the very thought. "Like, not at all," she added.

My cracked heart flipped. I was glad that she felt that way about us. Sad that she had to. Sad that any child would feel they had to walk on eggshells for fear of being removed from their home, their foster parents replaced, a new unknown.

I vowed to live up to her trust in us. I couldn't promise that she would never leave me: DCF can move children who are wards of the state without notice. But I could promise that *I* wouldn't leave *her*. Not for making a mistake. Not for anything.

—⁂—

As Janine's discharge date drew near, a meeting was convened to decide where she would be going to school. She had been at Clinton Care for nineteen months now, most of them school months. She had briefly attended public school but found it overwhelming. Most of her time had been spent in a therapeutic school where teachers from the local public school came to the Clinton Care campus and taught small classes. She had spent ninth grade entirely in a therapeutic setting.

Janine was a smart girl. A straight-A student. She hated the therapeutic classroom. She felt the classes were simplified to the lowest common denominator. The only class she found at all challenging was physics.

"I'm getting dumber and dumber the longer I stay here," she complained.

But she needed the support of the therapeutic setting. Ben thought she would need that environment after discharge as well.

Janine had been pulled from her classes to attend the meeting. She was coming home on a weekend pass with us directly after that. So we threw her overnight bag into the back seat of my car, then chatted casually on the walk from her dorm to the administrative offices where the meeting would take place. We waited outside in the early summer sun. One by one the other attendees arrived. I knew Janine's DCF worker and her supervisor and her CASA worker. And, of course, I knew Ben. Other faces were unfamiliar. We filed in and took seats around an oblong table in a room without air conditioning. I saved Janine a seat beside me. As the last person entered the room and the door closed, I realized that Janine was not with us. I asked Ben what was up. He nodded at Rhonda, the DCF supervisor.

"I just feel like all the grown-ups in the room should be on the same page before we bring Janine in," she told me, a saccharin smile pasted onto her face. Ben shrugged, like he'd had this fight with Rhonda before and knew it was a losing battle.

"She already feels like she has no voice in the process," I complained.

"That's okay," Rhonda said, still smiling. "She doesn't have to like it. We're the grown-ups."

I didn't agree, but I could see her mind was made up.

The meeting began. Sara, the education coordinator for DCF, had been doing some investigating and had decided that Hillsboro High, which Janine had her heart set on attending, was not a good option. The school had 1500 students as opposed to Newburyport High School's 500. My own experience with Hillsboro High was limited. I had visited it once when I first opened my pediatric practice to introduce myself to the school nurse and see where my patients spent their day. It was a chaotic scene. The campus was large. The halls echoed at startling decibels. I knew from Mariah who had friends who went there that fights broke out regularly. I had to agree, it was probably no place for someone as fragile as Janine.

Sara continued. "Newburyport High has what they call a sub-separate therapeutic classroom," she reported. "There's an adolescent adjustment counselor available to students throughout the school day. Janine could use that space to re-group if she were struggling. Some kids take all their classes in this alternative classroom. Others are mainstreamed for most of the day."

I had to admit it sounded like just the kind of support Janine needed. Other voices at the meeting chimed in. Michelle, the girls' CASA worker, Janine's teachers at Clinton Care. Ben. Everyone was in agreement. NHS could meet Janine's academic needs and mental health requirements.

So it was done.

"You don't look very happy, Mrs. Bornstein," the education coordinator observed.

"So we've basically just made this decision without Janine's input and now we're just going to tell her," I said.

The group looked around the table at each other. Finally, Rhonda responded.

"Like I said, we grown-ups..."

"I just think Janine would have really benefited from hearing the discussion and having a voice."

Michelle spoke next. "Sometimes someone with a great deal of anxiety can't really make decisions for themselves. Sometimes they need someone else to decide for them." I had certainly seen this to be true with Janine. Ben had had to forbid her from going to her Nana's that Thanksgiving when he could see her anxiety was sky high. I'd had to nix a visit to her cousin Amy's for the same reason.

But this was different. This was her life. Her future. It was true, most 15-year-olds weren't making their own unilateral decisions about where to go to high school, but they were likely in the conversation. This just felt wrong.

Rhonda nodded at Ben who opened the door. Janine took her seat beside me. I patted her knee and gave her a weak smile. I felt guilty for not speaking up for her sooner. As Rhonda outlined all the reasons that everyone felt NHS was her best option, Janine sat stone-faced. Her leg started jack-hammering up and down like it did when she was struggling to keep her emotions in check.

"So that's it," she said flatly. "I get no say in this."

I couldn't even look at Rhonda. My heart pounded with anger. This was exactly what I had feared. This child had had no say in her life for so many years and we were letting it happen again.

Janine probably didn't realize how little choice Saul and I had in all of this. We were not technically even her foster parents yet. All these months of family therapy and home visits were a good faith effort on our part. No contract that had been signed yet. We had no formal role to play.

I agreed that Newburyport High School was the best choice for Janine. I knew that she would eventually see that, too. I knew that wanting to go to Hillsboro High wasn't about choosing what was best for her. She would hardly even know kids there anymore; she had been out of that school system for so long. For Janine, it was more about loyalty. It was where she grew up. Where her mom still lived. To choose not to go there probably felt like a rejection of her family. Of her past. Here we were giving her no choice at all.

As we walked to the car, I tried to put my arm around Janine's shoulder, but she shrugged it off, then walked two steps ahead of me. She slumped into the passenger side of my car. I turned on the engine and let the AC blow but I didn't move from the parking space.

"I'm sorry," I told her. "Rhonda insisted we start the meeting with just the 'grown-ups' in the room," I said using air quotes. "She promised you'd come in for the last half of the meeting. I realized too late that everyone else had already made the decision for you." I waited. Janine did not respond. I turned in my seat to face her.

"Look at me," I said. She did, the cool AC swirling her curls around her face. "I promise you. Right here. Right now. That this will never happen again if I have anything to say about it. I promise you, I will always—always—fight for you. To have a say in your life. To have a seat at the table."

I thought I saw a tiny smile waft across Janine's face momentarily. I put the car in drive and pulled out into the tree-lined street.

"Thank you," she said, then turned up the radio.

Janine's completion of ninth grade coincided with her discharge from Clinton Care. After 19 months in the program—she was nearly the record-holder for length of stay—and after ten months working with Saul and me, she was finally coming to live with us full-time. We were finally going to actually be her foster parents.

"I just want to *live* here already!" Janine would complain through gritted teeth time and time again on passes home. Sunday nights had become a struggle to get her re-packed and into the car and back to the program by curfew. She'd hurl herself into my arms, letting her feet fall out from under her so I was holding her entire body weight. She'd procrastinate. She'd pet her cats. She'd forget hygiene products necessitating numerous trips up and down the stairs.

Section I—In the Beginning

The prospect of being completely and solely responsible for this fragile child was daunting. We had learned much about eating disorder: its origins, its manifestations, its treatment. We just didn't know what it would be like to live with this illness full-time.

A large part of Janine's treatment had been spent constructing what is called a trauma narrative. Survivors of trauma often have recurring memories or thoughts that they have no way to process. In therapy, writing their story—literally listing on paper the incidents they've been through and how they feel about them—helps them to organize their thoughts and make sense of their feelings. Also, reading it over and over again in therapy was supposed to desensitize them to its harmful effects.

We knew Janine had been working on this narrative for months. Most kids write a few paragraphs or a couple of pages.

Janine had written 11 sheets.

On both sides.

Single-spaced.

We also knew that Ben had told her she could share it with us or not. It was her call. We knew the basics of Janine's trauma. When she chose to read the entire story for us, we learned new details. Janine sitting with her father in the ICU rubbing his feet until 2 a.m. Waking up at five o'clock at home, feeling empty. Learning later that this was the exact moment he had died. I knew that the girls had been physically removed from their mother on a very emotional day. I hadn't realized that it had happened on Valentine's Day.

I learned things that made me ashamed that as the girls' doctor I did not know. Her mother abusing her father. Faces slapped. Objects thrown. All witnessed by the girls. Her father grabbing his daughters and leaving once, only to return later that same day. How could I not have known that was going on? Even if no one told me, shouldn't I have seen it in their eyes?

Janine's narrative included Mariah's hospitalization with that rare bacterial infection and how scared she was that she would lose her. All her relationships—father, mother, sister—were for different reasons tenuous and fraught.

There was humor in her narrative as well. "I'm shedding like

Figgy and Toby," her dad had joked about going chemo-bald, referring to the family cats.

Janine tried to make positivity come from the reading too. She had learned from a priest that her father had promised he wouldn't die on Mariah's birthday.

"I will always keep my word," she vowed.

Jimmy had taken the girls bowling even when nausea kept him housed in the men's room for most of the time.

"I will push through adversity," Janine concluded in her narrative.

Janine's mother hadn't believed her for a long time that a family friend had abused her.

"I will always believe my children," Janine concluded.

When she was done, she sat quietly, her pages in her lap. She looked us each in the eye, as if gauging our response. There was a palpable solemnity in the room. This girl had just shown us her most painful past. It felt like a "This is what you're getting, are you ready for it?" moment. There was no turning back now.

"Thank you for that." Saul broke the silence. "That was very brave."

"You're welcome," Janine replied earnestly.

"Thank you for trusting us," I concurred. "You made yourself very vulnerable just now."

"You're welcome," she said again, her sober blue eyes piercing mine.

The residents of the program typically destroyed their trauma narratives after reading them in a ritual called a destruction ceremony. Some kids set fire to their words. Some drown them in water. Janine chose to shred hers into tiny pieces, stuff them into balloons and set them free. I hoped that Janine's chosen method of "destruction" revealed a basic optimism about her.

Ben had bought balloons and rented a helium tank. Saul and Ben and I all helped take the small squares of Janine's past and tuck them carefully into brightly colored latex. We took turns talking with funny helium voices, laughing at each other, which felt good after the somber reading. Underneath all the light-hearted frivolity, I wondered if Janine and Ben were realizing what was just now occurring to me: This was going to be the last time they saw each other. Nineteen months of therapy and hard work was coming to an end.

When we were done, we took the balloon bouquets—two groups of a dozen or so each—and walked from the dorm to the parking lot behind the administrative buildings. It was the same walk we had taken the week before for Janine's discharge planning meeting. Staff gathered. Macy. Sara. Ben. We all surrounded Janine. She giggled. We counted to three and Janine flung the balloons into the air. One group fluttered effortlessly away, over the treetops and out of sight. The second bunch got momentarily tangled in wires over the dorm rooftops, then soared. We all stood shading our eyes from the piercing June sun, watching until the last bright speck of color was no longer visible.

"Well, Janine. How do you feel?" one of her counselors asked.

Janine smiled, looking content and composed.

"Relieved," she said with a definitive nod.

The congratulations that staff bestowed on Janine sounded sincere and were surprisingly consistent in message. "You're going to do great things," was the gist of every single wish for her.

Mine, too. She was bright and determined and had so much to give. Everyone who had ever taught her or cared for her or loved her could see her enormous potential. I only hoped she could see it in herself.

We packed up the two cars. Saul and I had driven separately anticipating moving nineteen months' worth of living. Bins of winter clothes, bags of dirty laundry. Hair products. School work. My guitar. Games we'd bought Janine to pass the time when we had to visit her in the conference room on med protocol. Framed pictures of treasured friends. Ceramic projects made in art class. A Harry Potter wand that rumbled when its handle was squeezed, which happened each time my car took a right-hand turn.

Throughout the ride home, Janine was quiet. I couldn't exactly read her mood. Not nervous. Not depressed. Not ecstatic either. If I had to choose a word that described what I saw when I looked at her face next to me, I would say serenity. Or maybe maturity. She knew this was the next huge step in her life. She looked ready to take it.

We walked into the house lugging bins and bags and boxes. Homer barked excitedly. Janine patted herself on her stomach, inviting him to jump up on her which he obligingly did.

"That's right. I'm home," she told him. "For good. We're all home now." I smiled wordlessly at Saul, the way we used to smile at each other when the boys were small and doing something cute.

We walked into the kitchen where Janine stopped, her breath catching. Saul had ordered a big bouquet of flowers, just as he had when Mariah had joined our family.

"They're beautiful," she murmured, taking the 2×2 envelope from its plastic perch, fingering the card.

"Go ahead. Read it," Saul prompted.

She read. *"Dr. Seuss once said, 'People are weird. When we find someone with weirdness that is compatible with ours, we team up and call it love.' Welcome to our weirdness. Love: Saul, Carolyn, Mariah, Homer, Figgy and Toby."*

"Oh," she gushed. "I'm gonna cry."

"Turn it over," Saul said.

"There's more?!" she squeaked.

Saul nodded.

"It takes courage to believe the best is yet to come," Saul had written on the back of the card. This time she didn't read aloud. She just collapsed into our arms in a big family hug. I hoped we all had that courage.

In the Throes

SEVEN

Boarding the Struggle Bus

I always anticipated some regression. Some back-sliding. Janine had been living with her eating disorder for three years now. She had been in residential treatment for 19 months, supported by professional staff 24 hours a day, seven days a week. Now it was just us. I felt as ready as I could be for this next phase of her treatment: coming home. I didn't expect that all would go smoothly. I just wasn't prepared for how insidious the relapse would be—so subtle as to be missed, until it was almost too late.

Janine was, of course, off her meal plan when she came home which meant she was plating her own food: deciding what to have for breakfast, making her own sandwich at lunch, serving herself portions she felt were appropriate for dinner.

It was painful to watch.

She spread her tuna fish as thinly as a stingy layer of mayonnaise on her bread. She'd ladle out what looked like a reasonable serving of soup, contemplate the contents of her bowl for a few seconds, then dump half of it back into the pot. She'd take a tiny helping of rice, then surreptitiously mash it around on her plate to make it look like it was more than it was. And of course, she'd pull the irregular edges of her turkey or cheese from her sandwich so that the contents were even with the sides of her bread, leaving the scraps on her plate.

Eating disorder was always in Janine's head, telling her she was fat, ugly, didn't deserve to eat. You could see her inner struggle in her furrowed brow, her bitten lips, her shaking leg, as she tried to thwart the enemy within.

One evening we enjoyed a dinner of grilled chicken, sweet potatoes and zucchini out on the deck. We kept the conversation going, trying to keep Janine distracted. She finished her meal with not one morsel left on her plate. I was so proud of her. As we cleared the table and I put together a plate to take to Mariah at work, I packed only two slices of grilled sweet potato, not the three that Janine had eaten.

"Did I eat too much?" she wailed. "I ate too much! I'm so fat!"

While we certainly had the support and expertise of Janine's nurse practitioner and therapist, no one seemed to understand what it was like actually living with this brutal disease. Even as a pediatrician with a good deal of knowledge on the topic, I still could not have foreseen the death grip this disease had on its victims nor predicted the enormous toll it takes on the families who love them. And, of course, no one had the magic wand to wave and make everything better.

We saw Melody, Janine's nurse practitioner, at Children's Hospital our first week home. The medical assistant in bright purple scrubs gestured cheerfully for Janine to step up on the scale. When she started to face the digital read-out on the back of the scale, the MA shook her head and turned her finger in a circle, indicating that Janine should back onto it.

"Not blind weights again!" Janine protested. I was relieved. At Clinton Care, when Janine began being informed of her weights, she did not do good things with the information. She skated along the razor edge of the lower limit of her goal range, always slipping over into med protocol territory. Now she felt like she was going backward, not forward, in her treatment.

"I haven't had blind weights in like forever!" she complained. Melody listened patiently. "Ben said not knowing our weight makes us anorexics *more* anxious," she tried again. Melody nodded sympathetically, but she never told Janine her weight.

When we finished our visit, Melody had us cancel the two-week follow-up appointment Ben had made. She thought an appointment in a month would be fine. It felt validating. We must be doing something right. Melody hadn't told me Janine's weight either, but she didn't seem alarmed.

The same thing happened at Janine's intake meeting with her new therapist, Tessa. Ben had scheduled us for weekly visits. Tessa thought every other week visits would be adequate. It gave me some measure of self-assurance that her team thought we could handle this more or less on our own. Still a small voice worried in the back of my head, were they too confident in us?

The subtle signs of Janine restricting—the smaller portions, the pulled-apart sandwiches, the paper-thin tuna fish—eventually became not so subtle instances of outright refusal. I could always get her to eat, though sometimes she'd refuse what we were having, heating up a veggie burger in the microwave instead.

I tried to take the long view. The honeymoon was definitely over; that was clear. I knew this was Janine (or, more specifically, eating disorder) pushing back. Testing limits. Figuring out boundaries. What we would put up with and what was over the line. Maybe she was even still trying to figure out what was over the line with me and Saul, if we were really in it for the long haul. We tried to reassure her.

"We're not going anywhere. We're going to pull you out of this thing. Because that's what families do. We pull each other along," Saul told her.

I was less optimistic, to the point where I felt like I was fending off hopelessness constantly. I had to keep telling myself: *Okay. Worst case scenario: she loses weight. She goes back into a program. We re-group. We try again.*

"Do I look like a slut?" Janine asked us one day standing in the kitchen wearing ripped jeans and a crop top. We stammered something about how she always looks beautiful to us. She told us that at Clinton Care, if she thought she looked good in an outfit, she wouldn't eat for the whole day, afraid that she'd gain weight and not look good in it anymore. The same thing happened with her hygiene ritual. If she showered first thing in the morning and decided she looked okay in the mirror, she wouldn't want to eat breakfast. If she showered after breakfast and decided she was fat, she wouldn't eat lunch or dinner. She told us that, since being discharged, she still heard those awful voices in her head; they just weren't as constant, loud or controlling as they used to be.

"They're still there," Janine explained. "Just quieter."

I tried to discern all the things that could trigger Janine to restrict. I eventually learned that this was a near-impossible task.

Triggers were everything and everywhere. One day she declared out of nowhere, "I'm not eating lunch." I used my best skills to try to figure out what had brought this on.

"Gee, you came home in a pretty good mood," I started. "Was it something that happened after you got here?"

"It's something *you* do every single day that's triggering me," she offered cryptically and accusingly. I was stumped.

"Well, I certainly don't want to be triggering to you," I said, still trying to see what I was missing. "I can't change something if I don't even know what it is that I'm doing."

We sat across from each other, me with my cold beet soup and potato salad, her with her untouched sandwich. She fidgeted in her chair, pulling strand after strand of hair from her head. (Trichotillomania was an obsessive hair-pulling habit that was part of the anxiety that often accompanies eating disorders. Janine had bald spots in her scalp and short broken hairs along her temples from her constant pulling.)

"Look," she said sternly, staring down at her plate. "I know you're dieting or something. I can see that." She looked up at me and continued. "You don't understand. I have to be the person who eats the least around here and I'm not. I have to be the thinnest and I won't be if you're on a diet."

I was flabbergasted. I was definitely not dieting. For the past year I had been eating sandwiches with her every day for lunch even though I was not a sandwich person. I much preferred eating leftovers for lunch. Wheat berry salads, tabbouleh, chowders. I had tried to be as supportive as I could, eating bread and meat for the past year. But I thought it was time for me to go back to my routine. Now I was learning that my routine was triggering.

"I just don't really like sandwiches that much," I told her honestly. "I've been doing this every day for a year now." I paused. "For you," I added, hoping she'd at least appreciate the effort.

"You didn't finish your muffin this morning either," she went on, undeterred by my magnanimous confession.

"But I ate like half the batter," I said, trying to take a lighter tone. "That was like a whole muffin right there." She looked dubious.

"It was delicious," I added.

I smiled.

Janine did not.

With all the gravity of a funeral director, she slowly dispensed a dollop of hand sanitizer into her palm. She then worked her hands in rapid circles round and round like a housefly. I wondered if she was counting the strokes. When she was done, she picked up one half of her sandwich, her head dangling morosely over it. She nibbled the crust, set it back on her plate and sighed deeply.

"Always making the decision to get fat," she murmured, more to herself than to me, obviously echoing the shaming voice of her eating disorder in her brain. Anguish settled in my gut as I watched my child's inner turmoil.

"If you could live inside my head for just one day," she half-whispered, as if reading my mind.

"I'd love to," I told her, grabbing her hand. I meant it. I wanted to share her pain. To feel what she felt.

"No, you wouldn't," she said sadly.

I slid my chair around the table and sat down next to her. I laid my head on her shoulder.

I thought about my own father, long since gone from this world. When I was a child, I was at the doctor's office, having a plantar wart burned off my foot. It hurt so much. I was crying in pain, trying not to, but wailing, nonetheless. My father had a death grip on my hands, staring straight into my eyes, his own face contorted to block his tears.

"If I could be in that chair, I would," he promised me. And I could see from the hurt in his face that it was true. Even though the acid was burning my foot, it was searing his heart.

"Yes, I would," I whispered to Janine, hoping she would understand. "I truly would."

On the day Janine was discharged, we had had a phone meeting with Ben and DCF to "make sure a plan was in place," as Rhonda put it. We went over Janine's appointments with her nurse practitioner and therapist and reviewed our summer plans for her (which at this point was just theater camp). We made a date for her DCF social worker to come out to the house. After we hung up, Ben casually announced to us that he was planning on maintaining "an ongoing non-therapeutic relationship" with Janine. I didn't even know what that meant. He also declared he would be picking her up some time next week to go to a local amusement park. Although I found this all vaguely unsettling, I said nothing.

Then at home one day, Janine was texting with someone and laughing. I asked her who she was talking to.

"Ben," she said casually, her face remaining glued to the screen.

"Wait, you have his cell phone number?" I asked.

"Yeah. He gave it to me," she responded, not even looking up from her phone. "Oh, and we're hanging out next week."

Just like that. Hanging out. With her ex-therapist. A professional making plans with a teenager by texting her directly, not even going through her foster parents. My vague unease grew into full-blown alarm.

I talked it over with a couple of my friends who were therapists. Everyone agreed. This was definitely not right.

Saul and I sent Ben an email asking him to please go through us if he wanted to see Janine. He promised he would, though he continued to text her. I asked if his supervisors knew that he was planning on maintaining this "ongoing non-therapeutic relationship" with his ex-client. He assured me they did. I asked if they knew he had given Janine his personal cell phone number. Again, he said yes. I asked to speak to these supervisors. I learned he had two. I sent them both emails. Only one responded to me.

She told me that, as it turns out, Clinton Care did indeed have a rule against therapists giving clients their private cell phone numbers and against therapists being an "ongoing support" for their clients after discharge. But these supervisors had made an exception for Ben and Janine because Ben had seemed so "desperate." I remember thinking what a strange word choice that was. It seemed to me that if a therapist was "desperate" to maintain a relationship with a client, that should be a red flag in and of itself and probably the exact reason why those rules existed in the first place. This was also Ben's first real job right out of graduate school, another reason to apply the appropriate rules, in my opinion.

When I confronted Ben (again by email) asking why Janine had his private number, he said he had given it to her "in a moment of weakness." Again, an odd choice of words.

"She was having a bad weekend," he wrote. "I relented."

He made it sound like he was blaming Janine. As if she had been pestering him for his phone number and broken down all his defenses. Like she was a schoolgirl with a crush instead of a patient with medical needs. It seemed like a coward's excuse: blaming the victim.

I knew exactly what weekend he was referring to. Janine had attended a cousin's wedding with her family. We had prepared for it during numerous therapy sessions.

"Let's identify someone at the wedding who can help you if you're struggling," Ben had said. Janine wrinkled her brow in thought and bit her lip.

"What about Nana?" Ben offered. Her grandmother had had a lot of education about eating disorder at the program. But I knew she still didn't understand this mystifying illness. Maybe it was a generational thing. Nana was still firmly in the Nancy Reagan-esque "just eat" camp.

"I don't think so," Janine decided.

"What about Mariah?" Ben persisted. I had heard enough "I just want to live my life" complaints from Mariah to know she wouldn't want to babysit Janine at a party.

"She doesn't care about me," Janine reported.

"She loves you, Janine," I said. "She just doesn't know how to help you sometimes when you're struggling." I looked at Ben. I was about to suggest one of the girls' aunts. Neither had been educated about eating disorder or been in therapy with Janine, but her aunts loved her and I knew they'd want to help.

"Can't I just call the Bornsteins?" Janine finally asked Ben.

So that's exactly what Janine had done: called us keening from a closet somewhere in the church, "I'm an outcast. Nobody's talking to me. Nobody loves me. And I'm not eating that giant slab of meat!" Saul was frantic listening to her wails. He tipped the phone sideways between us so that I, too, could hear her distress.

I took the phone from him. I tended not to get sucked into the rabbit hole of self-loathing that Janine sometimes took us down. I tried a different strategy, deflecting her complaints and re-directing her to more positive notions. The next time Janine declared no one loved her, instead of just countering with "*We* love you" as Saul had, I hyperbolized with every cliché I could think of.

"You're the apple of my eye!" I told her. "You're the sunshine in my day! You're the moon in my sky!" I could hear Janine's sobs turn to quiet sniffles. I looked around the kitchen.

"You're the Coca-Cola on my counter," I joked.

"I'm the cuckoo in your Cocoa Puffs," she played along.

"Exactly!" I shouted. "That's what I'm talking about!"

"No, wait," Janine interrupted. "If I'm the cuckoo in your Cocoa Puffs, then that means I'm crazy."

"Yes!" I yelled. "And I'm the cuckoo in your Cocoa Puffs, too!"

She laughed. "Yeah, you are."

"See?" I said. "You belong in this family."

She giggled, then sighed. "Yeah. I really do."

She must have called Ben that day, too. But instead of encouraging her to come to us for support, he gave her his cell phone number. Not encouraging her to use her new skills to cope with her anxiety. Not encouraging her to rely on us, her foster parents, for help. Keeping her tied to Clinton Care. Tied to him.

As angry as I was about that whole situation, the more predominant emotion I felt was sadness. It was sad that Ben didn't have enough faith in himself as a therapist. Faith that he had gotten Janine to the point where she could safely be discharged and make this huge transition to a new home. Sad that he didn't have faith in Janine, either. Faith that she would be able to continue making progress in her recovery and continue furthering her trusting relationship with us. But mostly sad that he had no faith in us.

Of course, Janine knew none of this. For those days that Ben and his supervisors and I had been emailing back and forth, Janine continued to talk excitedly about "hanging out" with Ben. I had not been told of any change in plans by either Ben or his supervisors, so I said nothing. Still, I wasn't surprised when I opened the door that afternoon to see Ben and a woman I assumed to be one of his supervisors on my stoop. They looked like they were attending a funeral, all solemn-faced and head-bowed. The woman introduced herself as Kate.

Janine had heard Homer barking and the door open. She came up behind me.

"What's going on?" she wanted to know.

"Where can we talk?" Kate asked me, ignoring Janine's question. We went out onto the back deck. It was a warm July afternoon. No one took me up on my offer of iced tea.

Ben's head hung in shame. He avoided all eye contact with Janine, even as he apologized to her. For his mistakes. His poor judgment. His bad choices.

Kate apologized, too. For sanctioning this ill-advised arrangement. Together, they told Janine that there would be no ongoing relationship with Ben, non-therapeutic or otherwise.

Janine listened to their apologies, her face stoically set. At the end, they asked her if she had anything she wanted to say to them.

She said no.

Then she said yes.

"I just find it very ironic that the one person who helped me the most is now abandoning me like everyone else."

She quietly walked into the house, the screen door slapping gently behind her, leaving the grown-ups on the deck. In the end, I think Janine behaved like the most adult of the three of them.

The sad thing was, it didn't have to be that way. Janine didn't have to feel abandoned. If only Ben had allowed their professional relationship to be just that. Professional. She would have moved on, remembering him fondly and hoping he would be proud of her. Now, here he was, one more abandonment in her life. I saw my own irony in the situation. Janine was being abandoned by the very person who had first taught Saul and me about attachment.

EIGHT

Together, Alone

It was almost a full year after we'd first started working with Janine when she said, "I love you" for the first time. Spontaneously. On her own. First. Not in response to an "I love you" from me or Saul. We were at the beach with Saul's brother and his family. Janine was having a bad body image day. She told me she had put on her bathing suit at home that morning and thought, "Yeah. I can do this." Now, walking along the shore she said, "I don't know what I was thinking."

"When is my weight ever going to proportionalize?" she asked me.

"What do you mean?" I asked. "Like when will your height and weight be the same percentile?"

"No," she answered, looking confused. "I mean when will my body fat be evenly distributed instead of all going to my stomach like it does now?"

She pinched a meager fingerful of her abdominal skin, then let it go in disgust. It was so hard to know what to say to that. I gave the rote answer I learned to give in therapy.

"That's a distortion."

Like so many other times on this journey, I really wanted to climb into her body to see what she saw. Get inside her head and think her thoughts with her. Settle into her heart and feel what she felt. Just like my dad had with me in that office chair, I thought that if only I could understand Janine's angst and distress from the inside out, perhaps I could help take some of it away.

On our walk, Janine saw a young woman with a tattoo on the back of her right shoulder. Her pace slowed and she grabbed my arm and leaned over to whisper in my ear.

"She's an anorexic," she breathed.

72

"How do you know?" I asked.

"That's a recovery tattoo on her back."

I'd seen the symbol before: two wavy lines variously interpreted as a heart or a woman's body and meant to symbolize strength and courage and love. This woman didn't look very recovered to me. Her limbs were thin, and despite the temperate day, she seemed to be hugging herself for warmth.

"I just want to go up to her and say, 'Me too,'" Janine whispered.

"Go ahead," I encouraged.

"What if she yells at me?"

"I'll punch her out," I joked.

She laughed and cautiously walked over to the young woman and pointed gently to her tattoo. I couldn't hear their conversation, but they high-fived at the end of it and Janine skipped back to me, seeming satisfied.

When we got back to the blanket, everyone was noshing. I pulled out the Kashi bar I had brought for her and laid it on top of the cooler. She took it and threw it back in, slamming the top shut. The Kashi bar was the snack she herself had packed that morning. Now I offered alternatives.

"Cherries?" I asked.

"No."

"Watermelon?"

"No."

"Yogurt?"

"Double no! That poster in your office says that two to three servings of dairy a day are healthy. Yogurt would be my fourth serving!" she shrieked. I honestly couldn't even picture the poster Janine had in mind. I have lots of informational brochures for patients tacked up on bulletin boards here and there.

"You have anorexia, my girl. General nutritional advice doesn't necessarily apply to you," I explained. "You also have osteopenia. You need your calcium and vitamin D."

Finally, Janine reached into our bag, dumped some hand sanitizer on her palms, rubbed it in furiously, then reached back into the cooler, carefully unwrapped the Kashi bar and started taking small

73

nibbles. I breathed a sigh of relief. She then abruptly stood up and started chasing a flock of seagulls, running in large lazy circles with airplane arms, like a child. She was laughing in between bites. *Okay,* I thought as I watched her run and run. *Burning calories as she's taking them in.*

I couldn't complain, though. She was eating the snack.

We were sitting side by side on beach chairs. Everyone else was body surfing in the waves. I tipped my face to the sun and absent-mindedly played with her hair like she liked me to, twisting her curls around my fingers, then letting the locks fall. She rested her head on my shoulder.

"My girl, my girl," I said, patting her cheek.

That's when she said it.

"I love you."

"I love you too," I said. It would be the first of many exchanges we would have over the years, but this one was special. This one was first.

She tilted her face up to me and went on. "Have you ever had this experience," she said. "Where you're surrounded by people who love you and you love them and you just feel so overwhelmed with love, you just want to," she paused, struggling for words, "caress them?"

"Oh, you're having a B of C," I replied.

Janine sat up and turned in her chair to face me.

"A what?" she shrieked, as if appalled that I had reduced her profound emotional epiphany to a couple of letters.

"When Saul and I were first living together, he'd catch me staring at him sometimes and say, 'What? What are you looking at?'"

"I tried to explain it to him," I told Janine. "It was something like what you're talking about right now. Feelings you don't really have words for. I called it a burst of closeness. Over the years, Saul reduced it to a B of C. He'd see me looking at him with that look and say, 'You're having a B of C right now, aren't you?'"

Janine nodded, now feeling understood.

"Well, when I feel it," she said. "And I mostly feel it with you guys because you're the ones I'm mostly with, I just want to hug you."

I thought back to Ben and his gaping wound theory.

"Well, when that urge strikes, you should just go for it," I advised. And she did.

I breathed it all in. I breathed *her* in. The smell of coconut tanning oil on her skin. The feel of her thin strong shoulders in my arms. Her flyaway curls wrapping like pea tendrils around my face.

I think she was trying to tell me that it was okay now. It was okay to hug or touch. To ask for the comfort we need. Not worry so much about opening a wound or crossing a line. I think she was telling us that that's what she needed from us sometimes. Sitting here now, on a warm summer day locked in a salty embrace, maybe she was giving me what I needed too.

At the end of the summer, we decided to take our first family vacation. Saul's brother owned a home in Costa Rica and he was lending it to us for a week. The girls had never been out of the country before so we had to go before the judge to be allowed to get them passports.

"Where will you girls be going?" Judge Newman asked them.

"Costa Rica!" they both beamed.

The judge's eyebrows shot up and a kind smile spread over his face.

"I've never been there," he told them. They grinned at the thought of being worldlier than the judge they had been appearing before since the state took custody of them years ago.

The afternoon before we were to leave, Mariah and Janine wanted to go shopping for last-minute travel-sized toiletries and other sundries two teenage girls thought they might need in the Central American rain forest. I was busy packing myself so I didn't hear my phone ping with two text messages from Mariah. When I checked it a few minutes later, my heart sank.

I've been in an accident.

I'm going to the hospital.

I tried not to panic. After all, if she could text, she couldn't be that bad, right? But where was Janine? Why wasn't she texting me too?

Section II—In the Throes

With trembling hands, I called Mariah's cell phone. I anticipated Mariah's voice, shaken, scared. Instead a man who identified himself as a Newburyport police officer answered.

"Don't panic. They're both awake now. We're still at the scene. We don't know the extent of their injuries yet."

I panicked. If they were both awake now, that implied that at least one of them hadn't been awake before. This law enforcement officer was telling me, "We don't know the extent of their injuries yet," but he was not part of that *we*. That *we* was the medical community, *my* community. Doctors and nurses. The EMTs who were probably checking out my girls right now. I needed to get to my community. I had to get to my girls.

I called Saul and then raced to Clara Barton Hospital. As I parked my car, I saw two ambulances pull up side by side in the emergency bays. That had to be them. I ran over to the backs of the vehicles. Mariah's stretcher came out first. I grabbed her hand.

"I'm here. I'm here," I told her. She burst into tears. I kissed her hands. The EMTs pushed her gurney into the ER. Then came Janine. She had an IV running. Her skin, normally pale, was an extra shade whiter. I grabbed her hand, too. It felt like ice.

"I'm here. I'm here," I told her. She didn't respond. She was staring straight up at the sky, oblivious to my words. Now I was crying. Why didn't she hear me? Could she see me?

I followed them into their cubicles even though I had been told to stop and register them with the clerk at the window. I had learned my lesson about following the rules. I had waited obediently behind the glass to register my son Neil all those years before when he and his girlfriend Trista were hit by a drunk driver. Trista's mother Mary had sailed past me, desperate to reach her daughter. I would not be the bad mother again. Waiting behind the glass only keeps you from your kids.

Saul soon arrived. A police officer tried to fill us in on what had happened.

"Single vehicle accident. Car vs. telephone pole. This one was out until the paramedics arrived," he said, gesturing at Janine.

"Mariah was texting," Janine said, suddenly coming to life after being catatonically silent. The officer, Saul, and I just looked at each other. No one said a word. I smoothed Janine's hair. Unlike Neil, whose traumatic brain injury was sustained with no discernible external injury—no cut, no bruise, no dirt, no glass—Janine's hair was sticky with oozing blood and a purple bruise was beginning to bloom and swell on her cheek and around her left eye.

They CAT scanned her head. There were no signs of brain injury. They also x-rayed her chest and pelvis. No broken bones anywhere. She was showing more signs of life, asking for her shoes, her phone, her sister. I shuttled back and forth between the two girls. Mariah was scared. I tried to reassure her as best I could.

"You'll be okay. I'm right here."

They scanned Mariah's head, too. She, too, was spared a brain injury. These girls were lucky.

The police officer had told us that neither teen was wearing a seat belt. This was no time for a lecture, but it surprised me so much because in our household, cars don't move until everyone's buckled up. What had happened?

Janine attempted to explain.

"You know how I watch you eating and won't take a bite until you do?" she began. I had honestly never noticed that before. I nodded for her to continue. "Well, that's how it was with my seat belt. I put it on automatically like I do with you. But when Mariah didn't have hers on I thought, well, it must be cool to not wear a seat belt, so I undid mine."

A nurse was in the room adjusting Janine's IV fluids and setting her up to have her scalp laceration repaired.

"I've worked here for 20 years, Janine, and I can tell you that people's injuries are always worse when they don't wear their seat belts."

Janine took this in for a moment, then concluded, "Then this is all my fault," employing her go-to response of internalizing everything gone wrong. I stroked her sticky curls and reassured her, "It's not your fault."

I began thinking of our trip tomorrow in more and more wistful terms, convinced this was just not meant to be.

As if reading my thoughts, Janine began keening, "I want to go to Costa Rica."

"We have to wait and see what the doctor says," I told her.

"I just want to have fun," she wailed, dry-eyed.

Joe Hull, our friend who played Mother Ginger in *The Nutcracker*, was the ER doc on that day. He stapled Janine's head, cleared both girls' films and handed me a suture removal kit.

"Take them out in five days," he told me. "You know what to look for." He shrugged his shoulders and gave us the go-ahead to travel. "She just has a concussion. I see no reason to keep her."

Janine was overjoyed, but it terrified me to think about taking these two battered girls two thousand miles and six hours away from home. I *did* know what to watch for, of course. But I felt that by piling neuro checks and wound inspections on top of eating disorder management, it was turning into more than I could (or wanted to) take on during a family vacation. Weren't vacations supposed to be relaxing? What was going to be relaxing about this?

Joe expedited our discharge and home we went. It was almost 8 o'clock now and nobody had eaten. No one was hungry. But one of us had to eat.

I fixed sandwiches for me and Janine. Janine tried to refuse. I told her quite honestly that if she didn't eat, we couldn't go to Costa Rica. She just sobbed into her plate. There were real tears now.

"I want my mom," she cried. "I want my dad."

There were so many times taking care of these girls where I'd felt inadequate, second rate. Like a poor substitute for a real mom and dad. I'd always done my best, of course. But there were times when my best just wasn't enough. When I just wouldn't do. When the hole in their hearts felt like too big a well to fill. When they needed their parents. I hugged Janine and said lamely, "I know."

I called the girls' grandmother. I let her know what was going on. More than anything, I wanted her to talk to Mariah. Since we'd gotten home, Mariah had been angry. Slamming doors. Yelling on her phone. The police officer at the hospital had told us he suspected texting even before Janine made her comment.

"One car accident. Teenage driver. Probably texting," he'd told us in his tightly-clipped cop-talk.

Mariah had vehemently denied this.

"There was a truck taking up the whole road," she'd insisted tearily. "I had nowhere to go."

In the meantime, I got Janine to eat a little something (choke down between sobs was more like it). I iced her eye and put more Bacitracin on her staples. Mariah helped her get showered. Eventually both girls went to bed. We had hired a driver to take us to the airport. He would be here at 3 a.m. It was an ungodly hour when you've had the kind of evening we'd just had. We weren't even packed. In the silent house, Saul and I threw our clothes and toiletries into suitcases. We packed whatever we could think of that Janine might eat. Then we just crawled into bed and hoped for sleep.

Before Saul and I became foster parents, we usually took one big vacation a year. Sometimes our destinations were exotic: Thailand, Cambodia, Vietnam. Often, we explored our own national parks: Yellowstone, the Grand Tetons, Big Bend. Or we'd laze on Hawaiian beaches or Caribbean cruises. I always enjoyed the planning as much as the trips themselves—buying travel guides and searching the Internet for interesting restaurants to eat at or sites to see. Now, with a child with anorexia, vacation-planning had turned into stomach-churning angst.

The girls were so excited when we told them we were thinking of taking this trip.

"We're going to Costa Rica!" Janine would tell everyone, her thin, sweet face shining with excitement. I tried to let her enthusiasm infect me, but all I felt infected with was dread. Besides eating only very specific foods, Janine had a million other eating rules. A certain number of hours had to elapse between meals. Portions needed to be measured, re-measured and double checked. Hand sanitizer was a must. We had to have crossword puzzles available and play games during meals to distract her from the dreadful chore of eating. How would we manage all that in a foreign country?

I watched both girls for signs of worsening head injury, knowing it was unlikely given their normal CAT scans. Janine had a plum of a shiner on one eye. Mariah also had an ugly bruise that took up almost the entirety of one thigh. "Dios mio!" a zip line operator said upon seeing it. When the girls recounted the story of their fateful accident to her, she philosophized, "Well, that means God isn't done with you girls yet. You haven't fulfilled His plans for you."

Indeed.

Both girls proved to be quite adaptable. We rode horses through the jungle, took moonlit walks on the beach and watched lightning storms from our mountainside terrace. They were constantly snapping pictures of the lizards and scorpions, bugs and butterflies that lived among us. They managed better than I'd predicted without phones or malls or friends.

Janine initially did pretty well eating, too, considering the fact that the foods were foreign and the labels in another language. One venture out to a restaurant ended in disaster with Janine sobbing, "Eating out is fun for you but it's not fun for me" and refusing her meal. We weren't doing it because we thought it would be fun. We did it for practice. So she could live in the world someday. Our last few days there, Janine stopped taking her meds, restricted food and refused all snacks. We left the country feeling defeated by her sickness.

If her illness left us feeling demoralized, Janine's medical providers left us feeling abandoned and alone. It wasn't entirely surprising when we visited her nurse practitioner a few days after our return that Janine had lost weight. We recounted our rocky start to her: the car accident, the loss of consciousness, the staples, the black eye. We reviewed for her Janine's eating (or lack thereof) for the week: the laudable effort Janine had made by trying as much as she did in a foreign country, the eventual downslide into restriction and refusal toward the end. We agreed that given the difficult week, some weight loss was not unexpected.

We saw the nutritionist who made recommendations: milk with every meal. Adding in a morning snack. Janine's eyes glazed over, and I could see inside her. Inside her eyes to the eating disorder within saying, *This isn't happening.*

We made an appointment for the very next week to get Janine weighed again. As we pulled out of the driveway the next week to go to her appointment, we both looked at each other and said, "Snack!"

We had almost forgotten. I put the car in reverse and re-parked. Janine ran back into the house and came back with the lowest-calorie option she could find: a one-ounce box of Sun Maid raisins. I sighed.

As we pulled into the parking lot at Children's Hospital, I asked Janine if she wanted to take her snack in with her or eat it in the car. She rolled down her window and dumped the box of raisins onto the pavement.

Janine got out of the car and sauntered toward the clinic's entrance. I sat motionless in the driver's seat, tears in my eyes, breathing deeply and blinking slowly to keep them from running down my face in a full-on meltdown. Janine could ill-afford those calories lying uselessly on the asphalt. Finally, I exited the car and followed Janine up the wide staircase, colored squares of light from the stained-glass window throwing patterns on my feet as I climbed.

At the visit, we learned that Janine's weight remained unchanged. Ninety-one pounds the nurse had told me, unaware that she shouldn't, apparently. I breathed a small sigh of relief. She didn't lose.

Melody, the nurse practitioner, was dismayed. She shook her head and clucked her tongue and said unhelpful things to us.

"Janine, you've got to turn this ship around."

What did that even mean? How?

That's when I realized once again with a gut punch just how alone I was in all of this. Or, more accurately, we were alone. Saul and Mariah and Janine and me. We had a doctor and a nurse practitioner. Janine had a nutritionist. We each had our own therapists and our own social workers. Saul's brother Louis had recently started trying acupuncture on Janine and teaching her yoga. We had a whole team, for God's sake. But we were all alone.

I was alone.

Her doctors and nurses and social workers may have been able to list the facts about how to treat anorexia. Maybe they all could ace a test on eating disorders. But I was living with this disease every day. Hour by hour. Minute by minute. From meal to snack to meal. I knew what it was like to look into the eyes of eating disorder. The defiance. The food throwing. The swearing. The defeat. Being made to eat. Bite by bite. Crumb by crumb. Sip by sip.

Section II—In the Throes

These health care providers got to go home at night. Got to get away from eating disorder. Relax. Watch TV. Think about other things. I was in the throes of a mental illness that had us all in a chokehold. No vacation from it. No respite. No days off for good behavior. I once read about an older pediatrician who used to tell the parents of his young patients, "I am the professional. But you are the expert." I quote him often in my practice. Now here I was on the other side. I was an authority on Janine. A connoisseur of the bad behavior that came with this awful disease. Sometimes I felt at a complete loss as to how to live with it.

I felt I was being scolded by this nurse practitioner. Blamed. The head shaking. The hopeless look. I was angry. Did she not understand anything? Janine had needed the Jaws of Life to extract her from a car wreck. She ate foods she couldn't name in Costa Rica: gallo pinto, dorado, patacones. She had lost weight, of course. But this week she had maintained that weight. Despite the looming start of a new year at a brand-new school with no friends yet. Despite secretly exercising again (three times in one day, Janine had told me). Despite all the demons who lived in her head shaming her, telling her she did not deserve to eat. Despite all that, she had maintained her weight. If Melody didn't see that as praiseworthy, I just didn't know what to tell her.

I steeled myself for the same chastisement later that week when we met again with Janine's therapist Tessa.

I sat in the waiting room, flipping through women's magazines and fielding phone calls from my patients. Finally, Tessa called me in as she usually did for the last five minutes of the session.

Today, it was the most helpful five minutes I had had since starting to work with Janine almost a year before. Tessa reminded me of things I already knew but was forgetting in the mounting stress of life with an eating disorder.

"Meals should be light. Conversation. Music."

I knew this. We had learned not to talk about weight or food at mealtimes. It could feel like ignoring the elephant in the room sometimes, but that was what was helpful to children with anorexia. It had led to a particular vigilance and a certain feeling of fraudulence during meals at our house: trying not to show my immense relief when Janine finally picked up her fork and took her first bite, all the while talking about how Fetty Wap's songs all sounded the same to me.

I knew all of this. But as Janine's weight had dropped over the summer ounce by ounce, pound by pound, I was scared. Instead of light conversation, I hawked her every chance I got.

"The nutritionist wants you to drink milk with your meals," I advised her one evening the week before during mealtime.

"I don't give a shit what the nutritionist wants," Janine had replied.

"That's what scares me," I confided. "That you don't give a shit."

I knew it was going against the rules. But desperate people do desperate things. And with Janine seemingly floating away, I was desperate.

"Also, Carolyn," Tessa now went on, "there's no blame here. It's no one's fault. It's just where we are right now."

Again, it was a helpful reminder of something I learned a long time ago. Don't blame the child. Her behavior was not her own. It was her illness that was in charge during those ugly dinner exchanges.

Saul and I knew this. We had learned to separate the illness from the child. We were even encouraged to name it.

Edie.

As in E.D.

As in eating disorder.

It wasn't our sweet Janine who regularly called me names simply for calling her to the dinner table. That was Edie. Edie who threw forks at my head for trying to coax her to eat. It was Edie who invaded Janine's body. Who set up shop inside her head. Shamed her into self-starvation with a constantly running negative loop of self-loathing: *Fat girl. Ugly girl. Unworthy girl.* We knew all that. Today Tessa went one step further.

"And don't blame yourself either," she told me. I took comfort in those words in that moment. But it wasn't me she was concerned with.

"You feeling bad just makes Janine feel guilty."

I hadn't thought of it like that before.

Her last suggestion was the most helpful of all. (I later learned that this one had been Janine's idea.) And it was this: Instead of expressing my worries and concerns at dinner or trying to guess at triggering behaviors I may have been unaware of, we would have a nightly check-in. After dinner and before bed. A time for each of us to say what had perhaps been on our minds, just waiting for the right moment. I loved it. I was confident that I could hold my tongue and not fret about portion size or milk not chosen if I knew I'd get to have my say later on.

That night, Janine and I had our first check-in. She went first.

"You want to know something?" she said. I nodded.

"It's not always *what* I eat, it's the *way* I eat that makes me anxious," she said, opening another tiny door into her illness. Trying to give me another small insight into what it was like to live in her head.

"What do you mean?" I asked.

"Well, like tonight. I had peanut butter and apple for snack."

"Right," I agreed. She had had this snack many times.

"Well, when I got to the last slice of apple and I still had more peanut butter on my plate to scoop up, I immediately became anxious that I had taken too much," she explained.

Eating disorder was such an exhausting disease.

I went next.

"I've been thinking," I began. Janine scootched a little closer to me on her bed. "I'm going to let the doctors worry about your weight," I said.

Janine cocked her head, lines gathering on her forehead. I held up a finger, asking for patience.

"And I'm letting the nutritionist worry about your calories," I went on.

"Huh?"

"And I'm going to let Tessa worry about your mental health."

"Jeesh," Janine complained. "What else is there?"

"I'm going to worry about us. I'm going to worry about this relationship," I said, pointing back and forth between the two of us. "Because this is what I can control." I paused, fighting back a tear.

"And this is what is starting to feel a little off track lately."

Now *I* scootched closer to *her*.

"And this is what's most important to me," I said, hugging Janine to me. "So, this will be my focus. This will be my job. Let everyone else do their jobs. I'm just focusing on us."

She smiled, then leaned her head on my shoulder. I thought our first check-in had gone pretty well. Yes, we were all alone, but we would be alone together.

NINE

Warding Off Demons

The rest of the summer passed slowly. Janine was now fifteen. She was getting weighed every couple of weeks. Each ounce of weight loss, even each week that she maintained her weight, was met with much handwringing from her doctors at Children's Hospital, though not much in the way of concrete suggestions. We did get some advice from her nutritionist—adding Carnation Instant Breakfast to her milk, putting oil on her rice, dipping her baby carrots in hummus instead of eating them plain—but they were all met with Janine's refusal. Not with the doctor in the room, of course. There, eating disorder stayed out of view, hiding inside Janine. But on the car ride home, Edie came out of the shadows.

"Wait, wait, Carolyn, please," she pleaded with me. "Can't I try just one thing before you make me eat more food?" I couldn't imagine what her proposition would be.

"You know how I tear the edges of the turkey and cheese from my sandwiches to make them even with the bread?" Indeed, I did. Janine had been doing that since the first meal she had eaten at our house.

"Well, can I *please* just try not doing that first before you make me eat more food?"

I didn't think a few strings of meat and cheese would add that many calories to her already meager intake. But when I talked with Saul about it later that night, his response was "This could be huge."

And he was right. I would later learn that all this trimming was what was termed "a behavior" and behaviors were to be discouraged. It was eating disorder's way of reducing its victims' intakes. If we could break Janine of that habit, we would be taking a big step forward.

Nine. Warding Off Demons

So we agreed.
Had eating disorder lost?
Or had I?

—◦◦◦—

As the first day of school loomed, Janine's anxiety intensified. We arranged for a tour of the high school in an effort to ease her angst. We met with the adolescent adjustment counselor, Miss Fine, who headed the academy (or the "alt room," as the special needs students called it). As it turned out, she used to be on staff at Clinton Care before Janine's time there. We met Wanda, the school nurse who seemed to have experience with eating disorder and knew all the right questions to ask.

"How will I know when you're struggling? How can I help you in that moment?"

She offered Janine her rocking chair any time she needed to "take space" and her microwave oven if Janine thought heating up her rice sock would help.

We continued to use evening check-in to try to process her anxiety and make progress with her eating.

"I really want to eat more variety," Janine told me one night. "Will you help me find something new to eat?" We settled on toast and egg for breakfast and soup and half a sandwich for lunch. The next day, breakfast went okay, though I heard Janine sigh, "That was hard" when she finished. When it came time for lunch, she was worked into a frenzy.

"Every can of soup has a protein, a starch and a vegetable, but they don't have amounts," she worried. "How will I know how much of each to eat? And I already had bread for breakfast. How can I have even half a sandwich for lunch? Ugh.... Just pour me an Ensure!"

If I was exhausted taking care of Janine, it had to be a thousand percent more exhausting being her.

At another check-in, she told us how, if she seemed to be struggling with a meal, she wanted us to say, "Let's step away from the table and talk." I had this idea in my head that once Janine stepped away from a meal, there would be no getting her back.

87

And that was my Achilles' heel. I was too afraid to push Janine, to confront eating disorder. Afraid that what small amounts she was eating would turn into refusal and zero intake.

I'd spent the summer despairing and doubting my ability to handle this disease. I felt alone and unsupported by the so-called experts. I tried to convince myself that we were just progressing at our own pace. That maybe Janine's recovery wouldn't look like the next girl's. That we were on our own path and we would get through this together. I'd been telling myself that I knew what was best for my child. *Taking walks will make her stronger! Being in nature is good for her mood!* Was eating disorder really laughing at us? Saying, *Ha! I duped Janine out of another hundred calories thanks to that sucker of a foster mom.*

The first day of school finally arrived and the anxiety that first morning was thick in the air. Janine came down wearing a dress I had made for her over the summer. We had picked out the pattern and fabric together. When it was finished and she was trying it on for me to hem, I had made a mental note to myself that it clung to her frame and made her look too thin. So the next time we were at Jo-Ann Fabrics picking out a pattern and material for me to make her a romper, she noticed that I was buying enough material for a size XS instead of the XXS she wore today.

"Thanks for saying I'm fat," she had huffed at the check-out.

Now I told her, "Aw, you're wearing the dress I made you."

"Yeah, the one you think makes me look fat," she muttered. I tried to ignore the comment.

She got her book bag and solemnly and stoically got into the car for Saul to drive her to school.

He called me as soon as he dropped her off.

"How did she seem?" I asked.

"Subdued," he reported. "At least she went in." He was right. The fact that she'd gotten in the door was huge.

I was packing Janine's lunches for her at that time, though she chose what she would have. On the second day of school, she stood in front of the open refrigerator door, acrylic nails drumming. I had taken Janine and Mariah to the mall for back-to-school shopping where they'd gotten their nails done and their eyebrows threaded. What ever happened to backpacks and pencil boxes?

"How about tuna fish?" I offered.

Janine shook her head. Her nails drummed louder. She was also "body-checking." This is a behavior where an anorexic checks the size and shape of her body either with a furtive glance at her reflection in a window, or a pinch of the skin to check for fat, or, in Janine's case, rocking her hips back and forth while feeling her protruding pelvic bones.

"Turkey?" I suggested.

She slammed the fridge shut.

"Fine."

I took out the turkey (two slices) and cheese (one slice), mayonnaise (one tablespoon) and bread (two slices) and made her a sandwich. Before I could wrap it in waxed paper, she grabbed the deli package.

"A serving is only one slice!" she wailed, even though she had eaten this exact same sandwich dozens and dozens of times.

"Just pack me an Ensure," she snarled.

I couldn't imagine her uncapping a liquid supplement in front of teenagers who probably associated the drink with the elderly actors they'd seen drink it on TV.

"How about egg salad?" I asked.

"How about you go to hell?" Janine (that is to say, her eating disorder) countered. By now she was in tears. I wrapped my arms around her. She crumpled into my hug. "Look," I said, "it's my day off today. You go get ready for school and Saul will drive you. I'll pack us both a lunch and I'll come to your classroom at noon and we'll eat together, okay?"

She dried her tears and nodded, relief on her face. She headed off to the laundry room to pick out an outfit from the dryer.

———∞∞∞———

At our next weigh-in, Janine was 88 pounds. She told Melody that she felt hopeless and worthless and that she didn't want to be on this earth. I didn't know what the magic number would be at which

Melody would tell us Janine needed "more support" (which meant re-admission to a program) but we had to be getting close. She suggested I make an appointment with a psychiatrist for a medication evaluation and return to see her in one week.

While Janine was getting dressed, Melody took me out into the hall.

"How are *you* doing, Carolyn?" she asked me earnestly. No one ever asked about me. My emotions started to burble up inside of me—my feelings of failure, of being overwhelmed, of wanting to give up. I started to tear up. I wanted to say *"terrible!"* I wanted to explain what it was like for me. Mothering someone who never got well. Nurturing the un-nurturable. Melody didn't wait for an answer.

"Do you think public school is good for Janine?" she went on. "She tells me there's nothing she likes about it."

I swallowed my self-pity. How silly of me to think anyone really cared about how I felt. I took a big breath and widened my eyes in an effort to prevent my tears from breaching their lid-levy, hoping they'd gone unnoticed.

I tried to answer her question. I thought about the ice-breaker Janine had told me they'd done in her English class where they had to come up with rock band names based on random words chosen from a hat. And how in science class they were asked to wander around the room "randomly, like atoms" until the teacher rang a bell. Then they had to ask the person nearest them three questions. She made friends with two girls in her chemistry lab and declared a third "definitely potential friend material." She loved her theater class and was thinking about trying out for the part of Dorothy in *The Wizard of Oz*. She reported walking to geometry class feeling like the new kid that she was, when she heard over her shoulder, "Hey, Janine." It was Jack, a kid she'd met at the summer theater program she'd hardly attended.

"No, I think she can handle it," I told Melody now. "I think it's good for her. It gives her structure. Keeps her busy. And she's making friends." Melody nodded. "Okay," she said. It was starting to make me feel like the expert on Janine again, though I still had misgivings about my own qualifications.

"What about her therapist? Do you want me to give you the name of a new one?" Melody asked. I was perplexed.

"Why would I?"

"Janine says it's like talking to a brick wall." I thought back to the sessions where Janine and Tessa came out into the waiting room laughing. How sometimes they didn't even include me at the end of the session. How Tessa had been the one person I'd found helpful since Janine had left Clinton Care.

"No, we're good," I told Melody.

I knew that all of the complaints Melody was listing just meant Janine was getting used to new situations and people, like her reporting her first experience on a home pass with us to Ben as negative, only to gradually come to see it as quite positive when we processed it in therapy.

No, I was sure of it now. We *were* good.

That evening was uneventful until just before bedtime. As snack time approached, I readied our plates: a bowl of chips for me, peanut butter crackers and milk for her. I called her into the kitchen. "I just want to finish my homework first." It seemed reasonable, but as the clock ticked past 9:30, I wondered if this was just a ploy by eating disorder to get out of evening snack.

Sure enough, when I heard the textbook snap shut, I hurried into the living room to reiterate that snack was ready. I was too late. Janine raced upstairs and started brushing her teeth, a sure sign that snack was not happening.

I picked up the bowl of chips, a palpable frustration rising in my throat. All the feelings of inadequacy I'd kept bottled up in front of Melody that afternoon came rushing back up my throat like hot acid. The tears I'd refused to cry now flowed freely. I lifted the bowl over my head, intending to toss just the chips themselves into the sink, thinking the act might release some of my anger at myself for not being able to get Janine to eat.

I let the chips go, but instead of just the chips flying, the ceramic bowl itself slipped from my fingers and shattered against the sink into a million pieces.

Mariah's dark head poked gingerly around the corner.

"Are you okay?" she whispered.

"Yeah, I'm fine," I lied. "I just dropped a bowl." I could tell from her face that she could see it for what it was. Me losing it. Me out of control.

As if I didn't feel badly enough about being a failure at turning around Janine's restricting, refusal and weight loss, now I was also the brutal freak of a foster mother who threw things and terrorized her charges. I stood there alone crying silent tears. Jagged pieces of china lay at the bottom of the dirty dish water among the soggy chips, the mess emblematic of this new low for me.

Who was I, even? I didn't recognize myself anymore. I generally had my mother's temperament. She was a true Southern belle, quiet and demure. Her nature was mine. I didn't ruffle easily. During residency the interns all wanted to be on call with me because I was unflappable in emergencies and showed no anger when things went south. But even with a thousand nights in the ICU, I had never been under this much stress. All my efforts to help and heal Janine fell flat. She was withering away before my eyes and I felt powerless to stop the decline. I was failing. As a doctor. As a mother. And I was angry at myself for that failure and ashamed of myself for my loss of control.

That night the girls had a sleepover in Mariah's room. Not unusual. But tonight, I wondered what Mariah was telling her sister about what she'd seen and heard. What kind of monster must they think I was? I couldn't bring myself to knock on their door. Clear the air. I just bottled up my shame and self-loathing and went to bed.

The next night I made a beautiful pasta dinner with mushrooms and walnuts and sage. Janine nuked a veggie burger and stuck it in a half a pita pocket. No side dish. No milk. She ate snack with no resistance that night. She must have been starving, though she would never admit to actually wanting food.

At check-in that night, I tried to take back the reins. I told Janine that we needed some rules. I told her that she had to be more consistent with after-school snack. Her lunch period varied widely at school from first lunch at 10:45 to third at 12:30. She frequently complained when she got home that either she had just eaten lunch so she wasn't hungry for dinner, or she had eaten lunch so long ago that

I needed to have it on the table ASAP. I promised to check in with her via text during the day to see what lunch period she had so I could better gauge when to start cooking.

"Thanks," she responded to my proposal.

Next, I suggested that if she did request an early dinner, she must leave the kitchen and engage in an activity until it was done. She could read or crochet or play her guitar. Her hovering while I cooked only increased both of our anxiety levels. She acquiesced.

We decided on an evening snack time and Janine agreed that she would take a break from homework to eat it. She seemed relieved at the structure I was imposing.

The next day after school, she kept me waiting. She was usually prompt, walking down the long front sidewalk alone to my car. Today when she finally tossed her book bag on the floor and plopped herself into the front seat, she smiled slyly at me.

"Aren't you going to ask me why I'm late?" she teased, adding, "You'll be flabbergasted."

"Okay, why are you late?"

"*I* was socializing," she announced, lifting her chin and flipping her hair. "Actually, I socialized all day," she said. She went on to tell me that everyone in her history class had laughed at her jokes. That a popular girl in her chemistry class had picked her for a lab partner. She sang me the songs she learned in Spanish to memorize the colors and the days of the week.

"Oh! Wait! That reminds me!" She turned to face me. "What song should I sing for *Wizard of Oz* try-outs?"

I felt sustained in that brief instant. I was glad I had told Melody we were good with public school. These small shining moments were so few and far between, I tried to hold them tight in my mind, literally squeezing my eyes shut and knotting my fists to make the feeling last.

That night, I got ready for bed early. The Northern Lights were supposed to be visible in our area after midnight and my plan was to set my alarm and drive to Maudslay State Park to watch for them.

"You can't go to bed yet," Janine whined. "I need you for snack. I can't do it without you."

I recognized the pattern. Janine was afraid to rely on herself. Through all her time at Clinton Care, she was convinced that Ben was the only person who could help her. Now she was giving credit to me for her own internal abilities. She had everything she needed to do it on her own. She just had to trust herself.

I smiled at the irony. Here she was trying out for the role of Dorothy, a girl who always had the ability to get herself back home. She just had to believe in herself. And here was our own brave girl, strong in so many ways, convincing herself that she needed me, her deeply flawed foster mother, to get her through her evening snack.

"You had the power to go home all along," Glenda the Good Witch tells Dorothy in the play. "You just had to want it badly enough."

Janine could do this. She just needed to want to do it for herself.

TEN

Not Enough Tears
in the World

I was sitting at Logan airport on a Friday morning in September on my way to Minnesota. My seven-year-old great niece Emma had just lost her five-year battle with cancer. I was headed to her funeral.

It was also Saul's birthday.

Janine's weight had reached 85 pounds the day before I left. The doctor drew blood, did an EKG and gave me the phone number for Whitman Behavioral Care, a program specializing in eating disorders. It was finally time for that "higher level of care."

"I don't think they do intakes on the weekend," she told me. "Hopefully you can get her in next week."

I had called Whitman that very day and left a message. Sitting in the airport, I got a return call. I gave the intake worker all of Janine's information. I gave them Dr. O'Neill's phone number and fax so they could get the results of the labs and EKG.

"We have an opening today at noon," the clinician offered. But I'd be in the Midwest and I knew Saul wouldn't have help at the store until at least three o'clock.

"Can you do any later?" I asked.

"I'm sorry. Our latest intake appointment is at noon," she reported. "Could you bring her in on Tuesday?"

I could. I was planning on flying back Sunday night. I took the appointment and then called Janine's social worker Dottie to give her the update.

"Oh!" Dottie chirped brightly. "I think Rhonda's on the other line right now with Whitman requesting a bed."

Wait. A bed? What bed?

Panic set in. That wasn't supposed to be how it worked. From everything Dr. O'Neill had told me and from what I'd read on Whitman's website and understood from this intake worker, a clinician from the program interviewed the client and family, did their own vital signs, and reviewed the labs and EKG. Then *they* told *you* what level of care was needed. A hospital bed was the highest level of care. Residential was the next step down, where the kids lived in a kind of group home setting with their own therapy sessions and supports around meals. In the partial hospitalization program, they spent their days in the program but went home with their families at night. And in IOP or Intensive Outpatient Program, the kids still went to their own schools during the day. The program ran in the afternoons and evenings and involved ten hours a week of coached meals, family and individual therapy and structured classes for both kids and parents. I thought IOP would be perfect for our family. How was DCF just jumping straight to the highest level of care without even *seeing* Janine?

I demanded to speak to Rhonda.

"Oh, hi!" her voice dripped with false sweetness. "I was just going to call you!"

Bullshit, I thought.

"What's going on, Rhonda?" I got right to the point. "I have an appointment with Janine on Tuesday for an intake at Whitman. I'm headed to Minnesota for a funeral. Can't this wait until I get back? Why are you requesting a bed?"

Rhonda's more customary curt tone took over.

"I've been talking with Dr. O'Neill and she felt admission was urgent."

"That's not true!" I cried. "We were just there yesterday! She told me to make an appointment for next week, which is what I did."

I knew what was happening. Rhonda had decided that admission was what needed to happen. It was *she* who was conveying the urgency to Dr. O'Neill, not the other way around. I'd seen this from Rhonda before. This was her MO. It was Rhonda who was steering this ship, not Janine's physician.

"I don't even think she'll qualify for inpatient care right now," I added flatly.

"Well she *could* qualify," Rhonda now said cryptically.

"Based on what?" I shrilled. Heads turned at the airport gate. I didn't care. I was incredulous. Whitman hadn't even received Janine's labs to review.

"Based on the rapidity of weight loss," Rhonda replied, trying to sound clinical. I shifted in my hard plastic seat. I felt my fellow passengers' eyes on me. I tried to tone it down.

"But she has an appoint—" I whispered into the phone. Rhonda cut me off.

"Dr. O'Neill was very concerned," she asserted.

I could see this conversation was going nowhere.

"Dottie's going to pick Janine up from school today and drive her to Whitman," Rhonda announced.

"No!" I wailed, not caring who heard me now. "You can't do that! Janine has no idea this is happening. She'll feel betrayed by me. It will damage our relationship."

I thought back to the final meeting at Clinton Care where Janine was totally left out of the process of deciding her future. I promised her then that I would always advocate for her to have a seat at the table. Now we were being ambushed. She would be swept up by DCF and whisked off to Whitman while I was out of town, at the funeral of a child, no less. It felt so unfair.

"Janine's physical well-being is my concern right now." Rhonda took a holier-than-thou attitude. As if I were playing a game of Russian Roulette with my own child's health.

"Mine too!" I shrieked. My fellow travelers were glancing furtively in my direction. I wiped my eyes and looked at the clock. The flight attendant was boarding first class.

"Look, Rhonda, if she needs to be in the hospital, I'll take her there. I'll visit her every day. I'll work with her team." I was desperate. "We have an appointment Tuesday. It's four days away." My nose was running. My voice cracked. "Please."

My zone was boarding. I stood up, cell phone tucked under my chin, and grabbed my carry-on.

Rhonda cleared her throat.

"I am Janine's legal guardian, Carolyn," she reminded me curtly.

97

I sat back down. Hard. The wind was physically knocked out of me. I felt defeated. After knowing Janine for half her life, caring for her first as her doctor, now as her foster mom. Working with her for ten months, driving hours every week just to see her. Now my input about Janine's future was being ignored. I was not being trusted. I wasn't her legal guardian. So what was I? A mere custodian?

It was a pattern I would see time and again. DCF ignoring input from the people who knew these children best. Their foster families. DCF complying with metrics instead of listening to the families who love these kids.

"Rhonda, please. Just give me a couple of days," I begged, my voice now a whimper.

"Dottie's on her way, Carolyn."

I clicked off my cell phone. I left my bagel and coffee on the airport lounge chair, no appetite now. I found my seat and stowed my gear. I let the tears flow. My shoulders shook. No sound escaped my lips. I rested my head against the oval plane window, its surface cool against my skin. A dull drizzle had begun to fall over Boston. I traced a drop of rain with my finger, the rivulet mirroring my own grief. I was burying one child in the morning. Another was being ripped away from me at the very moment I was powerless to do anything about it.

With the few minutes I had left before I had to turn my cell phone off, I called Janine's alt room teacher and explained the situation. I wanted to give her a heads' up as to what was about to go down.

"Tell her I didn't want any of this," I sobbed to Miss Fine. "Tell her I love her."

In the end, Janine was recommended for the Intensive Outpatient Program, or IOP, the very program I had known would meet our needs as a family. She was not admitted to the inpatient unit as Rhonda had wanted. Saul called me at my hotel room in Minnesota that night to give me the news. Janine was scheduled to begin IOP in two weeks. She would undergo another intake with another set of labs and EKG, and I would be home to take her. We would do this together.

Ten. Not Enough Tears in the World

Dottie picked me up from school and is taking me to Whitman, Janine had texted Saul, seeming to accept the situation with ease. "I kept asking you guys to take over my meals for me," Janine told Saul.

Even if her statement was not technically true, it did in fact carry a weightier truth in it. Truth with a capital T. She told me at her next visit, sitting on the exam table waiting for her nurse practitioner, "I'm glad you took the bathroom scale away from me," then added, "Me. Janine." She was honestly and powerfully trying to separate herself from her disease. Trying to be seen. Trying to be heard. And I had failed her. Failed to see and hear what she most wanted me to know. That she was not cured. That she needed more help than we could provide. She didn't *want* it. But she knew she *needed* it. All her loud protests, all the acting out, the name-calling, the fork-throwing; that was all Edie trying to refuse to eat. Sadly, it was that loud balking voice that I had been listening to. Not the small clear one whispering, "Please help me."

Saul and Janine and I walked into Whitman on a cold October afternoon. We hadn't even made it four months on our own after discharge without Janine needing more support.

The building was still being renovated. The hallway leading up to the lobby was uncarpeted, black sticky tiles on the floor. The bottoms of the corridor walls were raw, awaiting baseboard. As we opened the frosted glass door, we were met by a smiling receptionist. Two carpenters in overalls worked on ladders stenciling "Whitman Behavioral Care" on the wall behind her.

We were invited to hang our coats up and put our meals in the refrigerator. We had been instructed to bring Janine a snack, which had to be at least 200 calories. Already, I felt the program's guidelines were helpful. No one at Clinton Care or Children's Hospital, not even the nutritionist, had ever suggested a minimal calorie count for snack before. For dinner, we would have access to a microwave oven, a refrigerator, dishes and cups. We were also to bring a typical family meal to be eaten communally.

Kristen, one of the clinicians, handed Janine a cloth Johnnie and motioned for her to go into the rest room. She left the door cracked open. She peed before her weigh-in. She did not flush the toilet. Staff needed to be sure that she did not make herself vomit to lower her weight. The scale in the bathroom was attached to a monitor with a digital read-out that lay on the floor just outside. Kristen recorded the number on a clipboard, then wrote it down on a yellow sticky note which she handed to us.

85.7 pounds. So this is where we would begin.

Joanne, our case manager, handed me and Saul a meal plan she had created based on Janine's current weight and her goal weight. Each meal and snack was divided into a certain number of grains, proteins and fats as well as vegetables and fruits. A caloric beverage was to be served with each. We were given a thick packet with examples of different kinds of foods from each category. This list would become my bible, my salvation and my bane, governing my life for the foreseeable future.

I absorbed all of it. I felt gratitude wash over me and confidence swell within me for the first time in a long time. I must have been smiling. I looked up to find Janine staring at me, a hollow look in her eyes. My smile disappeared. As was so often the case, what cheered me depressed her. Or at least challenged Edie.

Next, Joanne pulled out a page from Janine's chart with three columns: green, yellow, and red. She first asked Janine to name some foods she liked for the green column. These were foods we could serve Janine that would be relatively easy for her to eat. "Like" and "easy" were words Janine would never use in reference to food. I remember once serving spaghetti and meatballs with garlic bread. I noticed that Janine practically inhaled the fragrant miniature loaves. But the next time I offered garlic bread as a side, she refused.

"You *like* garlic bread," I said.

Janine had put her hands over her ears and closed her eyes.

"Don't ever say that I *like* something," she insisted. "I can't *like* food."

One morning, I forgot to serve her a fruit with her breakfast. She couldn't bring herself to point out my mistake—to simply ask for the fruit. Instead, she had to hint.

"I hear there's going to be a shortage of bananas this year," she said, eyes on her plate, head down.

"Oh?" I answered, not taking the hint. We ate on.

"Did you know they use these gases in an enclosed room to force bananas to ripen?" she tried again.

"Yeah, I've heard that," I replied. Then it hit me.

"Oh! I forgot your banana!" I handed her the fruit along with a knife and fork. We would later learn that cutting a banana into bite-sized pieces instead of peeling it and eating it by hand was "a behavior" to be discouraged. Right then, I was just glad she was eating.

Once when Janine and Saul were grocery shopping, Saul texted me.

We have a request for morning glory muffins. Text me a list of ingredients you need to make them.

I was thrilled and complied immediately. But by the time they returned home, eating disorder was once again firmly in charge.

"I should never have asked for them! Please don't make them!" Janine screamed as she ran upstairs. "It's like eating cake!" she shouted from behind her closed bedroom door, the words so obviously coming from Edie.

Now here at Whitman, she was being asked to name foods she liked. I held my breath, anticipating the same loud protests I had encountered whenever I had used that word. Instead, Janine was using a green colored pencil to underline foods from a list. Foods she liked. Yogurt. Granola. Sliced almonds. Bananas. I noticed they were all breakfast items, consistent with my observation that this was Janine's "easiest" meal to complete.

She went on to fill in her yellow list: foods she sometimes struggled with but could mostly manage to get through. Janine was looking more anxious. Her legs were crossed one over the other, the top leg motoring up and down like an oil rig.

Then came her fear foods. These were foods that were extremely difficult for Janine. They were foods to be worked up to. Foods we would gradually challenge her with. Once she ate them, however, they weren't simply a to-do box checked off. "They stay in the rotation," Joanne explained, directing her comments toward Janine.

Section II—In the Throes

By this time, Janine was completely shut down. Her motoring had stopped. Now her feet were curled under her, her face buried in her knees. Her soft brown curls, usually a nimbus around her sweet face, hung like a shroud over her bowed head. I reached out to squeeze her shoulder, let her know I was there for her. That I was proud of her for taking this huge, difficult step. Joanne caught my eye and shook her head. I withdrew my hand, confused. Was comforting not allowed here? Affection prohibited? Before I could get clarification, Joanne stood up. I guessed we were done here.

"So generally, after weigh-in, the kids go right into the conference room for snack," she explained. "Did you guys bring a snack for Janine?"

I nodded.

"Why don't you go get it? We'll meet you in there."

Saul and I reluctantly left our girl, crumpled in her chair and beginning to shake again. Having been advised that snack had to be at least 200 calories, we had brought a Clif Bar and juice. This was much more than the few raisins or Goldfish Janine was used to.

When we entered the conference room, Janine was seated at the table next to a teenage boy, the only other program participant thus far. She stared blankly ahead. I laid the Clif Bar in front of her and set the plastic tumbler of juice next to it. I fully expected her to stay catatonic or hurl the proffered items across the room as she had so many times at home. Instead, she ripped the wrapper open and robotically bit off a tiny corner, then took a small sip of juice. Joanne nodded toward the door, indicating we could leave now. She had this under control.

We learned the rules. Weigh-ins happened three times a week. If Janine did not consistently gain or at least maintain her weight, or if she had two or more unexcused absences, she could be asked to leave IOP and be recommended for a higher level of care, the partial hospitalization or residential programs. No one was allowed to use drugs or alcohol before or during treatment. Leaving the building during program hours was also not allowed.

While the kids were in their educational sessions, we parents had our own classes. The material covered would be parallel: the biopsychosocial theory about the origins of eating disorders, the nuts and bolts of dialectical behavioral therapy or DBT, the basics of addictive behaviors, a primer on nutrition.

And while our children were in their individual therapy sessions, we parents would participate in a support group, sharing what it was like caring for a mentally ill child. I was looking forward to interacting with people who were going through the same thing we were. Lastly there would be a family meal. We would all eat together in the dining room. We'd learn games to play to distract the kids while they ate. We'd observe the clinicians as they coached them to eat, gradually practicing the techniques ourselves. No behaviors were tolerated. No cutting food into minuscule pieces. No pushing it around on the plate. No tearing the edges off turkey sandwiches. Most important, every bite had to be consumed or they would have to supplement the unfinished meal with a bottle of Ensure.

During our parent support group, I met Lydia, mother of Gary, the only other kid in the program so far. He'd been suffering from his eating disorder for four years. While Janine had been discharged from a program but slipped backward and needed some extra support, Gary was coming at IOP from the bottom up (again) from hospitalization, to residential, to partial and now here.

"I don't know how much longer I can take this," Lydia admitted quietly. It would be a familiar refrain I would hear from many of the other parents I would meet. It surprised and comforted me at the same time. I had wondered the same thing countless times myself. But I was a foster parent. I literally had the option *not* to take it anymore. I could decide this was too much for me at any time. That *Janine* was too much for me. I could opt out of the whole thing. DCF only required ten days' notice. After that, I could literally send my problems packing. Now here were biological parents expressing the same weariness and frustration and angst that had been plaguing me for months.

These were my people.

The clinicians let us parents out a few minutes early so we could prepare our families' meals. Lydia and I took turns microwaving: me, hearty plates of homemade mac and cheese; her, individual Cup o'

Soups. I smiled at her. She sighed. She seemed defeated. After sharing her feelings in support group—her failure at getting Gary out of bed for school most mornings, her demoralization at being yelled at every day, the endless hours of travel, visitation and therapy in each of his last programs—she seemed all talked out. We set our places in silence.

Gary and Janine arrived in the dining room at the same time. Their eyes darted back and forth between our plates, no doubt comparing portions and calculating calories. We took our seats. Janine had to be coached by staff to even pick up her fork. She ate one macaroni at a time, hissing out of the corner of her mouth, "Why do I have so much more to eat than him?"

It was true. While Janine and Saul and I ate thick, gooey forkfuls of mac and cheese with a buttery breadcrumb top, Gary sat down to a Cup o' Soup and half a sandwich which he practically inhaled. He drained his glass of milk in one long chug, then took a great breath, like he'd just run a marathon. He pushed himself away from the table, scraping his chair loudly against the bare linoleum tiles.

"No one leaves until we're all done," Kristen reminded him quietly. Gary rolled his eyes and slumped down in his seat, his arms crossed over his chest in resignation.

Janine ate her meal to within two noodles, then laid down her fork. Kristen pulled a chair up next to her.

"You have two more bites, Janine," she cooed gently.

"What?!" Janine shrieked. "You gotta be kidding me! Did you see that mountain of food I just ate?"

"I'm done," she declared, pulling her knees up to her chest in her familiar shut-down position.

"I know this is hard for you," Kristen sympathized. "And you have two more bites. Then you can go home."

I did not yet recognize one of the crucial tenets of dialectical behavioral therapy at work in front of me. The idea that two things can be true at the same time. That we can hold these two truths at once. That something is hard. *And* (not *but*) you have to do it anyway.

Janine dug in her heels. This was one determined girl. I'm not sure Kristen knew what she was getting into with our little warrior.

"Just pick the fork up, Janine," she coaxed. "Just two bites."

All eyes were on us. Gary and his mother and the other two counselors sat at the table, unable to leave until we were all done.

Janine shook her head violently. *Was it worth it?* I thought. *Two bites? How many calories could that possibly be?* But obviously that wasn't the point. It was reinforcing the underlying expectation that we, the parents, were in charge now, not eating disorder. Janine would eat what she was served, no matter what.

I saw a tear slip from Janine's eye as she stared straight ahead, rocking now. Janine rarely cried.

"Let's take a walk." Kristen placed a gentle hand on Janine's shoulder. Janine shrugged it off, grabbed her fork, stabbed her two remaining macaroni and shoved them in her mouth so hard I feared she'd draw blood. Now she directed her wrath at me.

"There!" she screamed, unchewed noodle on her tongue. "Are you happy now?" she snarled, even though I hadn't said a word. Then she stormed out of the dining room toward the coat rack. Kristen followed.

Saul and I looked at each other and breathed deeply, relieved that the drama was over. Amazed that this program actually seemed to work.

IOP would come to feel like a full-time job to me. Saul and I split the routine. He took Mondays. My days were Thursdays and Fridays. Janine, of course, was on all three. And intense it was. Ten hours of therapy and instruction, driving thirty minutes each way three days a week, not to mention coming up with meals that could be prepped, packed, and reheated.

Although the work was intense, the big plus of the program was that Janine could stay in school. She was making friends fast. One day I came home from work to a living room full of teenagers, all friends from the academy.

"Who wants a snack?" I asked. Janine's mouth dropped open. We had not discussed this. All her friends' hands shot up in the air.

"Me!" they laughed in unison.

I looked at Janine and smiled. She looked relieved.

I went into the kitchen and set out peanut butter and crackers and V8 Fusions all around. The group tumbled into chairs and began to eat, hardly a pause in their conversation.

I maintained a cautious distance, puttering with dishes in the sink, glancing over my shoulder periodically, making sure Janine was eating. She was. She looked at me wide-eyed and I detected a slight incredulous shake of her head, as if she could scarcely believe other teenagers would eat without being forced to.

"Thanks Mrs. B.," Dylan mumbled through crumbs.

"Call her Carolyn," Janine invited. "I do." She shrugged.

Janine made friends outside of the alt room as well. Julia, a girl from her history class, would become Janine's best friend for life. Becca, Maddie and Emma rounded out the group. They did their homework together and went to high school football games as a pack.

Making friends, for Janine, helped solidify her place here in her new hometown. When she'd been traveling home on passes from Clinton Care, Saul and I had arranged experiences to help her feel like a part of the community. We helped her get a job volunteering at the local cat shelter. We signed her up for guitar lessons with a woman from a local band who would turn out to be much more than a teacher. Liz would become Janine's friend and mentor. Now, making friends on her own gave her a much firmer place in the daily life of Newburyport than we could ever arrange.

It also gave us ammo.

In IOP we learned that the key to restoring these children's weight was through consequences. Positive consequences for eating. Negative consequences for restricting.

"It sounds very punitive," Joanne told us early on. "And it is," she added flatly. "But it works."

We first tried the consequences approach on our own one evening when Janine proclaimed she was done with her meal even though her milk glass was still half-full and she hadn't even touched her salad.

"You have to finish your milk and salad," I pointed out. She had just eaten three slices of pizza. Before we'd started IOP, I would have been thrilled if she'd eaten only one.

"I'll do one or the other but not both," Janine announced.

"It's not a negotiation," I informed her.

"What are you gonna do, force it down my throat?" she scoffed.

"No," I answered. "But there will be consequences."

Janine laughed outright.

"What kind of consequences?" she demanded.

Saul and I hadn't really planned specifically what the consequences would be. I had to come up with something.

"If you want Julia to come over after school tomorrow, you need to finish your salad and milk," I stated firmly.

"What?" Janine shrieked. "You can't do that."

"I can and I will," I stated. "Now finish your dinner."

Janine snorted like a bull at a rodeo. She picked up her glass and drained it, then forked every leaf of lettuce into her mouth, staring me down all the while.

"There. I hope you're happy now, you psycho." I let the words roll off my back, pleased that these consequences had done their job.

After homework, when Janine sat down to evening snack, she very obviously and purposely excluded me. She turned her chair away from me and directed all her comments, smiles and laughter at Saul.

I tried not to let it hurt me. I told myself that this was just eating disorder being angry at being fed. I tried to focus on the fact that even though she was angry, she had eaten. She was letting us take charge of her meal plan. She was gaining weight. She was getting better.

I thought that after struggling with this disease and seeing its ugly face for over a year now, I'd be immune to this treatment by Janine. But it still hurt, and tears soon welled up in my eyes. I rushed through my snack and left the table. Janine followed me.

"Why are you crying?" she demanded. I didn't know how she could have even seen me with her back to me the whole time. So I lied.

"I'm not."

Saul had followed us into the living room.

"I think you hurt her feelings ignoring her through snack," he guessed.

"Well, that's just stupid," Janine now proclaimed. "No sense crying over spilt milk," she added snarkily.

"And when you're done with your little pity party here, I'm still having snack." With that, she turned on her heel and went back to the kitchen.

I knew it was Janine's way of trying to make amends. Inviting me to sit with her and eat snack. But my heart just wasn't in this. It was too busy breaking. I would learn in IOP all about using my "wise mind" in these situations. I would become skilled at setting aside my emotions and responding in a way that supported Janine and ignored Edie. For now, I just wanted to go to bed and lick my wounds. So I did, without so much as a good night.

The next morning at breakfast, Janine asked me if I had looked at my phone lately. I had not. After breakfast, I did. A text message from Janine had come in at 11 o'clock the night before.

I love you so much it is unbelievable and indescribable, it read.

I looked up to find her smiling at me. It still floored me that these two personas could occupy the same body. One so hateful and one this sweet. This was Janine's way of apologizing for that hateful demon who made her act in ways she despised herself for and did not truly understand.

We hugged and I kissed the top of her head, then sent her off to school with a gentle swat to the bum.

While consequences could be helpful, sometimes the outcome wasn't exactly a success. In fact, sometimes it was disastrous. Using friends as positive consequences had been effective, but if Janine had no plans, there was nothing to take away. No play date to hold over her. But her phone was her lifeline. Her connection to her teenage world. And it was something I thought I could leverage.

One evening Janine took one look at the dinner I'd made—wild mushroom risotto—and pulled a veggie burger out of the fridge to microwave. But the new expectation in IOP was that the parents were in charge. What was served was what would be eaten. No exceptions and no substitutions.

"Janine, if you don't sit down and eat the dinner I've made, I'll take your phone away. You can have it back when you eat."

She looked aghast.

"You can't do that," she countered.

"I can and I will. Now come sit down," I said firmly and calmly.

"I'm not eating that," she stated flatly.

"Let's play Contact," I said, trying a different tack. "Saul, you want to think of a word?"

"Sure," he said, playing along. "Okay, my word begins with an S."

Janine wasn't having any of it. She pointedly drummed her fingernails on the table and looked up at the ceiling. Saul and I played Contact, guessing at each other's words. Janine did not join in. When we finished, I poured her a glass of Ensure. She threw it in the sink. I didn't say a word, just went up to her room, grabbed her phone and put it in a desk drawer in my bedroom.

When Janine came up a few minutes later, she shrieked, "Where's my phone?"

I stayed calm.

"You can have it as soon as you drink an Ensure."

She ran past me down the hall into my room and grabbed my cell phone from my bedside table. She waved it in the air, cackling maniacally.

"Well, if you can take my phone, I'll just take yours."

With that, she pushed past me down the hall and into her bedroom and slammed the door shut.

I was a doctor on call. I needed my phone. It was the only tie between me and my patients.

I turned the handle and pushed on her door. It didn't budge. She must have been leaning her body against it.

"Janine, I need my phone. I'm on call," I said through the door.

Janine laughed.

"There, how do *you* like it?" she sneered. "You can have it back as soon as I get mine," she threatened.

I pushed the door harder. Janine still weighed under 90 pounds. Technically I should be stronger than her. I wasn't.

"Saul!" I called downstairs. "I need you."

He was already on his way.

"She's got my phone," I told him.

"I know. I heard," he replied.

I turned the knob again and together Saul and I pressed our weight against the door. It gave way in a rush as Janine leapt onto her bed, face down, my phone squarely underneath her.

"Give me the phone, Janine," Saul ordered calmly, trying to reach under her.

Janine drew her arms closer under her and said something soft and petulant into her pillow. I took her upper arm and tried to pry it out from under her. Janine started screaming.

"Get your hands off me! Don't touch me!"

Mariah came out of her room and around the corner.

"What's going on?"

Before we had time to answer, Janine popped up, threw my phone against the wall and ran downstairs and out the door. Barefoot. With no coat. Into the cold fall night.

"Janine, wait!" I called after her, but she was gone. Saul went after her on foot. I gave Mariah a quick recap of the argument. She immediately hopped into her car to look for her sister. After an hour, Saul came home to see if she had returned. When I told him she had not, he called the police who joined the search. After another 45 minutes of neighborhood-combing, they finally found her hiding in the woods at Mosley Pines right down the street from our house. Saul gave her his jacket and together they walked home without a word. I didn't know whether to hug her or strangle her. I did neither. Instead I called Mariah and let her know we had found Janine.

The girls slept together in Janine's room that night. I lay down on the floor in the hall with a blanket for a little while. I just wanted to make sure the girls got to sleep and Janine didn't try to run again. But all seemed quiet.

Getting ready for bed, as I brushed my teeth, I wondered what my world was coming to. Janine would have to get used to consequences because that was what the Whitman method called for and because they generally worked. At what cost, I wondered.

I would soon find out.

ELEVEN

The Sign

Twice in my life, I thought I was going to die. Once, when I was about thirteen, I was horseback riding with a friend when my horse Star got spooked by something and went from a gentle trot to a frenzied gallop. The force of his takeoff sent me swiftly off my saddle and onto the horse's rump. The reins slipped from my hands. I grabbed at Star's mane, saddle horn, stirrup—anything within reach.

We flew down a steep gravelly path that opened onto a grassy field. My body lost contact with the horse at every galloping step. I had no control. Star barreled at full speed toward the forest edging the meadow. Just when I thought we would go crashing into the trees, he veered abruptly at the last minute, sending me sliding further down his side. My legs lost their fragile grip around Star's body and were draped to one side, my Buster Browns scraping the grass, digging up divots of dirt like a bad golf swing with each hoof-fall.

As fast as this scene was playing out in real time, I was experiencing it in slow motion. As out of control of the situation as I was externally, inside I still felt calm. There was an inevitability to my circumstance that I could not deny. I just went with it. I remember realizing resolutely that I was going to die. I felt sad for my parents, but I was not scared.

The second time I almost died was when I was eighteen. I was sitting in the passenger seat of my boyfriend's van, probably unbelted. He was driving along winding back roads, pushing his van to go faster and faster, ticking off the speedometer readings aloud as we went.

"We're going 50," he told me, grinning. He floored it.

"Now 55." Another grin.

Just as he announced we were going 60 miles an hour, the road took a sharp turn and the van rolled once, twice, maybe three times. My boyfriend was a carpenter and I remember the sounds of his enormous toolbox as it flew through the interior, slamming against doors, ceiling, my knees.

Again, I was calm. I simply understood with great clarity at that moment that I was going to die. I was aware of the dire situation I was in. I could hear it and see it and feel it unfolding all around me. I was in a rollover car crash going 60 miles per hour with no seatbelt. But there was a disconnect. I was seeing my own end with lucidity and detachment. Still, I was not afraid.

The day after our cell phone consequence disaster, at about the time of day I would usually get a call from Janine if she needed a ride home from school, my phone rang. But it wasn't Janine. It was Saul.

"Janine's refusing to come home," he said. "Says she's afraid of us. Doesn't feel safe in our home. She told Miss Fine I tackled her. A 51-A's been filed. I spoke with the investigator. I'm on my way to the school."

I heard the words. I understood what each of them individually meant. But I was having trouble making sense of the story Saul was telling me.

A 51-A is an allegation of abuse or neglect and is filed with the Department of Children and Families. I had filed them many times in my career as a pediatrician against negligent or abusive parents. Now one had apparently been filed against us.

Though Saul had laid out the situation in stark detail, there was still an unreality to it that kept me from panicking. We had been working with Janine for over a year at that point. Her social workers at DCF had known me as her pediatrician for five years before that. We'd been in family therapy together at Clinton Care and now at Whitman. I fed her three meals a day, no small task at times. I scheduled her every doctor and therapist appointment and made sure she got there. Who could possibly believe we would ever hurt her? Who could believe that she was too scared to come home?

I hung up the phone. I threw in a load of clothes. I emptied the dishwasher. I stayed calm. I was unafraid. There had to be an explanation. This couldn't be happening. I did not panic. I somehow disconnected the analytical part of my brain—the part that knew that a 51-A was a very big deal; that there would be an investigation, interviews; that the mere fact of having one filed against us might even temporarily preclude our being foster parents—from my emotions.

I started cooking supper.

I remember feeling similarly disconnected the night I got the call telling me that Neil had been in a car accident. I had calmly put on my coat and shoes and set out for the nearby accident scene, convinced there had to have been some mistake. I had even considered taking my dog with me for the walk.

When something so horrific, so at odds with the reality of our lives the moment before, confronts us, our brains go into self-preservation mode, allowing us to function while biding our time for the truth to sink in.

I put the lid on the stew I was making and surveyed my clean kitchen.

An hour ticked by.

My phone rang again.

"We're coming home," Saul said.

"Janine, too?" I asked, needing confirmation. The worry that my protective brain had been keeping carefully in check now began bubbling to the surface.

"She's right here next to me," Saul assured me, then added, "The investigator is coming to the house, too. She said she'll be on her way shortly."

I hung up, only slightly relieved. On the one hand, the investigator couldn't be too convinced that Janine's alleged fear of Saul had true merit to it if she was allowing her to go home with him, alone and unsupervised in his car, no less. On the other hand, she was still on her way.

Saul, Janine and I sat at the kitchen table waiting. Saul filled me in on his interaction with the investigator. It turned out that when Janine had stubbornly stuck to her story of being tackled by Saul and afraid to go home, her teacher Miss Fine as a mandated reporter felt she had no choice but to file a 51-A.

"I never meant for this to happen," Janine now said softly, head bowed and shaking, eyes averted.

I stared at the top of her head. I felt empty, betrayed.

"Well, you complain when people don't take you seriously. Now they are," I told her darkly, adding, "Words matter."

"I'll tell them I'm sorry," she continued, eyes brimming with tears now. "I never meant for this to happen," she repeated.

But it had happened. Was happening. I, a pediatrician with hundreds of children in my care, was being accused of abuse and neglect. By a teacher. And by extension, by my own foster daughter.

My previously calm stomach slowly knotted up.

Janine was distraught. But I was in no mood to try to make her feel any better about what she had done. I was afraid. We might lose her. We might lose everything. My mind was starting down the rabbit hole of what ifs. What if word got out that a pediatrician was accused of child abuse? What if my patients left me? What if I lost my practice?

When Janine could see that I was mired in my own angst and not assuaging hers, she excused herself and went upstairs.

There was a knock at the door.

Homer barked.

Saul opened the door and invited in…

"Dottie?"

"I sent the investigator home," she reported with a wave of her hand, walking right by us and into the kitchen, where she'd been a dozen times. "I'm gonna finish this thing up myself," she said, hoisting her briefcase up on the counter, taking out notebook and pen.

I was confused and relieved at the same time. As much as Dottie and I had not seen eye to eye on any number of things, she was still a familiar face, and for that, I was grateful.

She took a seat with us at the table, shaking her head.

"Anyone can see this for what it is," she muttered. "Janine looking for a little attention."

Saul and I exchanged glances but kept silent. Dottie picked up her pen and began asking me questions. How had this all started? What was said? How did I remember the scene in the bedroom with the phone?

I answered her questions honestly, telling her what I remembered and how things had played out from my perspective. On the outside I was collected and cool even as my insides roiled.

Dottie was being so dismissive of Janine's allegation. So sure it was untrue. So convinced it had come from a place of teenage drama or petty revenge or, as she alleged, attention-seeking. She had always been dismissive. Of both girls, really. Janine once told me that Dottie had told her that she'd seen plenty of kids who had gone through far worse struggles than she had. The night Dottie had placed Mariah in an emergency foster home with a teenage boy, she looked at Mariah's low-cut blouse, then tugged at her own and told her, "Cover up," immune to the trauma of Mariah's experience. *("I've had some not-so-nice things happen to me in some of my foster homes.")* Perpetuating a blame-the-victim attitude.

Dottie finished with her questions, stuffed her notebook back into her briefcase and stood to leave.

"They'll see this for what it is," she assured us again. "You have nothing to worry about."

Though Dottie's dismissiveness bothered me, at the moment it was the only thing that was giving me any hope that things would turn out okay. I didn't know which emotion was stronger: gratitude for Dottie's hard-heartedness, or my guilt for feeling grateful for it.

For the next few weeks, we went through the motions of being a normal family. I packed lunches, paid bills, cooked dinners, and saw patients. Saul went to work. Janine and Mariah went to school. The 51-A was always on my mind. It would be weeks before the investigation reached its conclusion. Weeks before we would know the final outcome. Which meant weeks of my stomach being tied in a perpetual knot.

We never spoke about it again with Janine, but I knew she sensed our anxiety. Especially me. I became paranoid. I checked the local newspaper for headlines that never materialized. Even with Dottie's matter-of-fact pronouncement—*"they'll see this for what it is"*—I still worried. What if they didn't? What if they really thought Saul tackled Janine? Or worse? What if they believed she was afraid of us?

Janine had her own anxieties. For her, these were largely the same. We had now completely taken over feeding her and, according to Whitman's color-coded food list, were challenging her at every meal. Her lunchtime texts started at 10:30.

Why did you give me pasta salad for a side?!

I ignored that.

I am so done with you, it's not even funny.

I ignored that, too. My rule, enacted for my own sanity and self-preservation, was that if Janine's texts were cruel or vitriolic, I would ignore them. If they were more anxious, I would try to help her.

A bit later, I got another text.

I did it.

I texted back *Yay!*

I hate myself was her response.

Of course, through Whitman, I would learn that vitriol *was* anxiety. When parents would complain in support group about how cruel and mean our children could be to us, calling us names and throwing food, the clinicians would contort their faces into agonized expressions and say, "Wow. Imagine how much pain they must be in to act that way."

They even taught us that, in a way, their acting out so cruelly was actually a positive coping mechanism. That by turning their hatred outward, it helped them to not hate themselves, self-loathing being a main root cause of eating disorder itself.

It felt somehow validating for me to hear that. So often, I felt judged by people for "letting" Janine talk to us so disrespectfully. Dottie often scoffed at Janine's behavior.

"So entitled, that one," she'd say.

Rhonda, Dottie's supervisor, told us that Janine had to learn to be respectful to adults.

"That's just the way the world is," she noted, simplistically.

My own son Dan had once whispered to me after a particularly difficult meal, "Does she always treat you this badly?"

Everyone seemed to imply that we were letting ourselves be walked on like doormats. I felt that way myself, muddied and used. But Whitman shed a different light on these children's behavior. It was a manifestation of their illness. It was better than turning that pain inward and starving themselves. Absorbing this verbal abuse from our children wasn't us being passive. It was love at its most difficult.

I knew Janine hated herself when she was so awful to us. She'd apologize later, or text us some photo or saying. One time, she sent us a black and white photo of hands praying with an accompanying text: *Family is not the people you were born to, but the ones who were there for you.*

You're always there for me, she included in the text.

One day, I had an idea.

"Let's come up with a sign," I suggested.

"What kind of sign?" Janine asked, all in.

"A sign that says, 'I really do love you even though I'm being a total jerk right now.'"

Janine laughed.

"How about this?" she asked, placing a finger on the side of her nose.

"That's a good one," I said. "I can use it, too," I added, placing my finger aside my own nose. "'Cause I can be a total jerk as well."

And we did use it. A lot. One day after an especially ugly exchange where Janine called me psycho-bitch just for serving her a bowl of oatmeal, she marched dramatically out of the kitchen, only to return a minute later to, just as dramatically, place a finger on the side of her nose, then turn without a word and stomp back out of the kitchen and upstairs. It was kind of funny, but it told me that, even in those awful moments, sweet Janine didn't mean all those ugly names she called us. Sweet Janine was still sweet.

We didn't hear anything directly from the investigator about the 51-A. I asked my own social worker for progress reports but got the same dismissive answer as Dottie's *they'll see it for what it is.* That did nothing to ease my anxiety.

The weeks turned into a month.

For the last stage of the investigation, before DCF would either rule in or screen out abuse, they needed to interview Mariah. I dreaded it. For as many disagreements and arguments as the sisters had, they loved each other fiercely and had each other's backs to the ends of the earth.

What if Mariah believed Janine was afraid of us? Didn't feel safe in our home? What if she heard Janine interpret Saul's attempt to get my phone back as tackling her? What would she think? What would she say?

I never asked Mariah if she and Janine had discussed the incident. I never discussed the 51-A with her at all. Whatever the outcome, I wanted her answers to the investigator's questions to be the truth. If the investigator asked her if we had discussed the process with her or asked her what she was planning to say, I wanted her to honestly be able to say that we had not.

So I waited.

Mariah was a senior in high school then and working many hours at McDonald's. She had to meet with her own DCF worker once a month. She was loath to spend any of her spare time with the Department of Children and Families. It took four stomach-churning weeks for Mariah and the investigator to agree to a day and time to meet: at our home, after school.

A new investigator came to the door in a button-down, all-business suit and pumps, a briefcase in her hand. She shook my hand politely as Homer barked at our feet. There was no pretense of trying to make me feel at ease. I called upstairs to Mariah, led them both into the kitchen, then busied myself in another room, trying not to eavesdrop.

Mariah was loud and unambiguous.

"That's ridiculous!" she scoffed when asked if she thought her sister felt safe in our home. "Of course she feels safe here. This is our home!"

I breathed a small sigh of relief. Mariah wasn't done.

"It isn't even like a foster home to us. Carolyn was our doctor. She and Saul love us." Again she snorted. "Not safe. What a joke!"

I smiled. I remembered Mariah once musing to me when Janine would let only me pack her lunch, "This is Janine's comfort place now. It used to be Clinton Care. Now it's here. Home."

And now here was Mariah, giving her honest assessment of the situation. It didn't mean the end of the nightmare yet. It certainly didn't guarantee the outcome. It was just the best I could hope for at the moment and all I could ask of my girl.

The truth was, though, something inside of me broke just a little when Janine said she was afraid of us, when Miss Fine filed charges against us with the state. I looked at Janine with a certain wariness. I held back the full measure of my affection. Gave shorter hugs, maybe. Put less muscle into them, perhaps. I still held her, still placed my lips on the top of her head. But I felt a distance between us that was not there before and it was a space I knew I'd created.

I talked about my feelings with Saul, but he did not share my angst.

"She's just a kid, Cal," he told me. "She was just mad. She didn't get her way and she lashed out."

Whatever her motivation, if she did it before, would she do it again? I didn't want to spend my life second-guessing myself. Keeping my guard up with my own child. In my own home. For the first time since we embarked on this journey together, I questioned my commitment to it. Those first niggling misgivings I'd felt at the kitchen table with Saul all those months before had been effectively quelled all this time. I was all in. Now it wasn't simple qualms I felt.

It was fear.

Everything suddenly felt fragile to me. Unsettled. The very ground I stood on seemed to be shifting beneath my feet. I was wary and on guard. With one stubborn accusation—*I'm afraid to go home*—Janine had opened in me a cauldron of doubt. Everything that had come before—the name-calling, the tears, the throwing of food—I willingly endured all of it in the name of helping her recover. This felt different. The very viability of our nascent family felt on the line.

If anyone had a right to be circumspect, it was Saul. It was my husband who had been accused of tackling our foster daughter. It was he who would be justified in having second thoughts. But he had none. As it had been from the beginning, his commitment was full on. He waved away Janine's words as so much bluster.

"Dottie's right about this, Cal," he assured me. "I'm confident too. This will all turn out fine."

I tried to draw strength from him as I had so many times in our marriage. Through Neil's ordeal with his brain injury, through the deaths of both of our parents, I'd leaned on Saul. He was my ballast and main sail both. Keeping me grounded and pushing me on. But we were seeing this new event differently. Saul's attitude toward Janine's indictment felt as dismissive as Dottie's, though for different reasons.

Maybe they were right, Dottie and Saul. Maybe Janine was just angry at us for taking away her phone. Maybe it was as simple as that. Maybe this was all a vindictive act. Or maybe it was eating disorder balking stridently at these new consequences.

Or maybe Janine had been truly afraid. Maybe in that moment she had flashed back to some previous trauma. Some violence. Some abuse. I thought back to Ben's gaping wound theory. Janine's misinterpretation of touch. All kinds, perhaps. *Living with people who were not nice to me*, Janine had written in Ben's office outlining obstacles she had overcome. Maybe that obstacle wasn't as entirely overcome as she had thought. Maybe it would take more than a year of steadfastness, of showing up, of having her back, for her to really believe we were on her side. Not going anywhere. This felt like the first real test of our commitment as a family. And Saul and I, instead of being in our usual lockstep, were coming at it from different perspectives, Saul already there, on board, me many steps behind. Would we meet at the same point in the end? Together on an upright ship?

TWELVE

This Is How I Lose Her

With Whitman's support, I got very skilled at getting Janine to eat all her meals and snacks. I watched the clinicians as they encouraged their charges to take small steps.

"Just pick up the fork, Janine."

"Just touch the glass."

Those gentle instructions were expertly interspersed with light conversation.

"Those earrings are super-cute. Where'd you get them?"

I used time with her friends as positive consequences for completing challenging meals with red- and yellow-list foods. We took away those play dates if she refused. And it worked. So much so that sometimes I even smugly began to think of myself as The Anorexia Whisperer.

Janine seemed more invested in her treatment now. She still cried when she gained weight. She still started most meals complaining about portion size, or the number of fat exchanges. Sometimes she started out flatly refusing to start eating at all.

"Why do you have to challenge me so much in one day? Why do you insist on stuffing me like a turkey?" she'd cry.

Still, she was doing it. Slowly but steadily, she was restoring her weight and regaining her health.

———

I was finding the parent education program helpful and informative. The central tenet of treatment was dialectical behavioral therapy and the three main components of that were mindfulness, distress tolerance and interpersonal effectiveness. We learned to stay in the moment, to just observe thoughts and feelings as they developed, without judgment. We were taught self-soothing techniques we could use when we found ourselves in situations we couldn't control and didn't like. We learned to accept painful realities without suffering, sometimes called radical acceptance. We were encouraged to plan ahead and identify coping strategies in advance.

And sometimes it worked. For both of us. One afternoon, Janine was refusing to go to the program. I was distraught because, if she missed two sessions, we could be recommended for a higher level of care which would likely mean in-patient treatment. I wanted to scream at Janine to get her coat on. Tell her how hard I was working to re-arrange my work schedule and plan and prep meals to take for family dinner. I thought about DBT and realized this wasn't about me. It was about Janine and her struggles. I called Joanne and calmly told her I was having a hard time convincing Janine to come to the program and I would keep trying. Janine was in the next room, ignoring me. I called to her, using the language of DBT. "You're using your emotional mind in refusing to go, Janine," I said. "Maybe you could use your rational mind and say to yourself, 'If I miss more than one day at IOP I could end up back in residential. Then I wouldn't be able to go to school and see my friends.'" I waited. Nothing. I continued, "Or you could even try using your wise mind and say to yourself, 'Maybe I should go today. I need this. People are trying to help me here.'" I hadn't even finished that sentence when I heard her zip her jacket up and I knew we were good.

"If you so much as talk to me on the ride there, you'll be sorry," Janine warned.

That was okay. I'd take it for now.

Learning to stay in the moment was especially helpful. It was so easy to go down the rabbit hole of "what-ifs" when your child was starving herself. In one parent support session, a mother related the story of a particularly stressful family dinner. Not only was her anorexic daughter not eating, but she was being disruptive and distracting, going through the trash screaming, "I know these aren't my usual chicken nuggets!!" Her husband blew up and stormed out of the room.

Now, when her daughter refuses to eat, she thinks, "Then my

husband is going to come home and his head will explode. He'll have a heart attack and die on the spot and then I'll be left all alone to raise two teenage girls."

Wow. That was some rabbit hole.

I had my own tricks to try not to sink into deep despair when treatment was tough. Sometimes on the car ride to the program, Janine's anxiety would start ramping up and she'd start her name-calling early.

"Are you in competition with me to lose weight, you psycho?"

I'd try to ignore her fuming anger and instead concentrate on nature. I'd marvel at the cloud formations, appreciate the foliage, follow a soaring red-tailed hawk. Anything to stay in the moment and not get sucked into Janine's anxiety and anger.

The mother with the ticking time bomb of a husband rolled her eyes when I shared this in group.

"You can keep your fucking birds," she told me. "I've got real problems here."

I think she missed my point.

She was right in a way, though. Our children's suffering couldn't be ignored. And our own angst as parents couldn't be pacified with a blue-sky day.

One evening at dinner, all the other families were seated eating dinner and playing Contact, laughing loudly. Janine was refusing to even come into the dining room, much less eat. It was October 30, the day before her mother's birthday. She didn't have specific plans to see her mom as far as I knew. Either way, it would be hard for Janine. If she saw her mother and she was not in a good space (DCF euphemism for drinking or off her meds) it would not be a good visit. On the other hand, no visit would be hard, too.

I had made rice and a creamy chicken, mushroom and broccoli casserole. It was getting cold on the plate before Janine finally came in. She asked me to re-heat it, which I did. Then she started to eat. She was the last one finished. She finally put down her fork and pushed herself away from the table and sighed, seeming exhausted. A young clinician named Katie quietly pulled a chair up beside Janine.

"See if you can scrape up those last couple of bites, Janine."

It was a normal amount of food that a normal person would leave on their plate. But at Whitman they knew that eating disorder was manipulative and evil and if you gave Edie an inch, she would take a mile, and we'd come this far.

So I joined Katie.

"C'mon, Janine. If you just eat those last few bites, I'll go for an after-dinner walk with you when we get home."

She looked incredulous.

"Are you really gonna put that on me right now? After what I just ate?"

I immediately felt guilty. I was trying to do the right thing. Trying to abide by Whitman's rules. Follow Katie's lead. But look what it was doing to my child. Or was it eating disorder who was so distraught? I couldn't tell anymore.

Janine walked over to the window and started sobbing. Staff let the rest of the families leave.

I walked over to try to comfort Janine. I put a hand on her shoulder. She whirled around, her face within an inch of mine.

"Why do you hate me so much?" she hissed. I felt stricken.

Janine immediately left the dining room and started down the hall toward the exit.

Katie opened the door and called after her.

"Janine, are you all right?"

She got no answer, but I could hear Janine's sobs, loud and childlike, echoing down the hall.

"Janine! I can't let you leave until I know you're safe!" Katie continued.

She was gone.

"Is she safe?" Katie asked me.

I didn't know. I thought so. She had never actually tried to hurt herself before despite her mentions of feeling suicidal and her frequent "kill me now" refrains. I'd even heard her tell Ben once that she was feeling suicidal on one of their telephone check-ins on a weekend pass. He hadn't called us or had us bring her back to Clinton Care or take her to an emergency room. I had felt reassured, though ever watchful. When her new therapist Tessa had asked her during our very first intake interview, "When was the last time you felt suicidal?" Janine had answered, "This morning." Again, here was a mental health professional not recommending further evaluation. I didn't think I was wrong all those times for not taking her to the ER.

"I think she'll be safe," I told Katie now.

I grabbed my coat and followed Janine down the stairs and out the door into the cold October night. Instead of turning left toward where we'd parked the car, Janine had turned right.

"Our car's over here, J-9," I said, calling her by the funny name her friends sometimes used with her.

"I need air!" she shouted in between sobs.

I got in the car and drove over to her and opened the door. I sighed with relief when she got in. But she did not immediately put on her seat belt, which was odd.

"C'mon, put on your seat belt, my girl," I whispered gently. Then I started down the rabbit hole. What will I do if she doesn't put it on? Should I drive with her unsafe? Or would we have a showdown right here in the parking lot?

Halfway down the hole, I heard her belt click into place. I put the car in gear and edged out of the parking lot and onto route 95 North. Instead of feeling relief, I felt unease. Janine refused to tell her clinician she was safe. Now she had to be told to put on her seat belt. Maybe I was wrong. Maybe she wasn't safe. She was still sobbing.

Then she did something she'd never done before. She took her fist and started pounding herself in the head over and over again.

"Janine, please try to stop that," I gently urged. "That's just eating disorder mad at you for eating. But you did the right thing. You're getting better and I'm proud of you."

The pounding persisted. Now instead of striking herself with her fists, she was slamming her head against the door of the car. I was frightened. If she hated herself so much in this moment, what might she do in the next?

In anticipation of I didn't know what, I started to ease my car from the travel lane of this four-lane highway over to the slow lane. Before I could get there, the dome light went on and the car alarm dinged.

Janine had opened her door.

I braked desperately, veered sharply right, and came to a stop half in and half out of an exit ramp, just three exits from home.

Cars honked at us.

I thought we would die.

I put the car in park, still idling, and wrapped my arms around Janine, interlocking my fingers together at the level of her shoulders. She kept relentlessly pushing her body away from me and toward the door.

"You're okay, Janine," I whispered to her, my breath becoming ragged from the effort of holding this surprisingly strong girl. "I've got you."

My hold on her was slipping. As she inched her body toward the door, she was also dipping herself down, making herself small and harder to hold. My arms which were once around her shoulders now were against her neck and I was choking her. I managed to dial 911 on my cell phone with one hand. I was losing a bit of my grip on her with the other. I needed help.

"I have a suicidal teenager on route 95 North, exit 54!" I screamed. I was too far away from the device to hear an answer.

I thought I could hold her. I was a strong, healthy 58-year-old woman. Janine was an under-90-pound anorexic. She twisted her body into nothing until I only had her jacket in my hands.

I heard a rip.

I felt like I was holding my child over a cliff, a dark canyon, a raging river. If I let go, I was afraid she would die. Run out into traffic and kill herself.

I laid my cheek against her bony back and screamed. Loud. Constant. Primal. I never imagined such sounds emanating from my body. No words. Or maybe one word. *Nooooo!* Long and low.

My arms were losing strength. My neck and shoulders ached from the strain. Cars were still whizzing by us, honking, drivers yelling as they passed. I couldn't lose my fading grip just to turn on my hazards. So we sat in the dark and I held my daughter and prayed.

Little by little, I don't know how, Janine got first one foot, then the other out of the car and onto the ground. I strained to hear sirens. The state police barracks was just one exit away.

Where were they?

Janine's jacket fabric was tearing now, louder, more steadily. I was not so much letting go of her; she was leaving me.

Just like that runaway horse of my childhood, or my boyfriend's rolling van, I thought, *So this is how it ends. This is how I lose her.* I pictured myself having to tell the story to her family. Over and over trying to explain myself. *Honestly, I tried to save her. Please believe me, I did everything I could. I couldn't hang on.*

With that thought, she was gone. I released my seat belt and was out my door and behind the car in two swift moves. Janine was walking slowly, zombie-like, into oncoming traffic.

I grabbed her by the shoulders, yanked her backward, then tackled her and pinned her against the guard rail.

"I've got you. You're safe now. I won't let you go," I told her. "We're going to the hospital. You're okay."

She sobbed into my neck, the fight gone out of her now. Traffic whizzed by us, oblivious to our crisis.

I heard sirens.

Six state troopers surrounded our car. An ambulance arrived. I helped Janine into the back where she curled up in a ball on a stretcher. Two male EMTs asked me questions. Medications. Allergies. I told them about her trauma history.

"Don't touch her if you don't need to," I warned, invoking Ben's gaping wound message.

The ambulance pulled away. I could see the tops of the EMTs' heads as they tended to my girl. A police cruiser escorted me in my car to the local hospital. I knew I had to call Saul to tell him what was going on. For now, I just held tight to the steering wheel and howled into the night.

Clara Barton Hospital was busy. They put Janine on a stretcher in a hallway. She was placed on suicide precautions, so a uniformed security guard was seated beside her. She was curled up fern-tight with her face to the wall, not talking. Saul met us there. He and I stood beside her in the hallway, no offer of chairs.

The doctors performed a cursory exam. Their job was to medically clear her to be seen by Emergency Mental Health Services who would evaluate her and make recommendations for next steps.

When the young psychiatric clinician came to interview Janine, she didn't get much out of her. When asked why she opened her car door on a highway, Janine told her she just wanted to get some fresh air. The clinician and I exchanged worried looks.

Since Janine wasn't really talking, she took me and Saul to a quiet family room for our interview. We gave her some background on Janine. Her trauma history. Her father's death. Her mother's illness. And finally her eating disorder and the events that had led us there tonight. My pushing her to eat. Her despising herself for doing so. The refusing to say she was safe. The self-injurious head-banging. The opening of the door on the highway.

"How did you come to be Janine's foster mom?" she asked.

I told her how the girls used to be my patients. I told her about Linda bursting into my office unannounced with sick Mariah. I told her about finding out that Janine was languishing in residential treatment. That Mariah wouldn't unpack her bags at her latest foster home.

"I had to do something," I added.

"I knew there had to be a story there," she told me with kind eyes.

"I'm inclined to treat this as a genuine suicide attempt," the clinician told us after the interview. "I'm recommending an in-patient psychiatric placement."

I nodded. I had expected this. In fact, I would have been nervous to take her home after this night.

"Any possibility she could get into Alcott?" I asked, referring to Whitman's in-patient unit that specialized in eating disorders.

"I'll see what I can do," she promised and went off to make her phone calls.

Although I was frightened enough by Janine's behavior on the highway to call 911, and though I was relieved that they were recommending in-patient treatment and not sending her home, I still was not completely convinced that Janine wanted to die tonight. She hadn't bolted into traffic, after all. She had ambled vaguely toward it. She was in incredible pain. Such suffering. Such self-loathing. The sobbing. The head-banging. She definitely wanted her suffering to end. But I did not believe she wanted her life to end.

Maybe I was splitting hairs. Maybe it was just semantics. I knew she needed help. Maybe more than I could give her right now. I had naively thought of myself as The Anorexia Whisperer. Able to get her to eat when no one else could. Tonight I had failed her spectacularly. By pushing her to eat that last morsel of food, I felt like I might as well have pushed her into oncoming traffic myself.

Saul and I were led back to Janine. She hadn't moved a muscle. I rubbed her pink fuzzy-socked foot. She didn't respond. She must have been exhausted.

The bureaucratic wheels turned slowly looking for a psychiatric bed for a child in Massachusetts. Maybe it was the same everywhere. It was now after eleven o'clock. I told Saul to go home. He had to work in the morning. I didn't.

It was well after midnight when we learned that, because Janine had attempted suicide, she would be admitted to Thoreau, the general psychiatric ward at Whitman, not Alcott, the eating disorder-specific unit of the facility. I understood the rationale. I still felt Janine needed the specialized care of Alcott. We told Janine the plan. She remained shut down for the most part, only speaking once.

"Can you ride with me in the ambulance, Carolyn?" she asked.

"They won't let me," I told her softly. "I'll follow you in my car, okay?"

She nodded.

Thoreau at two a.m. was a depressing place. Visitors had to be buzzed into the locked ward. We were not allowed to have cell phones. These were confiscated at the desk when we checked in and returned when we left. Janine was limited even more. No pens. No pencils. No belts. The drawstrings had to be cut out of her sweatpants and hoodies. We were only allowed to visit for two hours each evening.

I signed Janine in and was told I could leave. I'd driven an hour and a half here to see her settled in and had spent all of five minutes with my girl. A staff member was leading her to her room.

Before she rounded the corner, she looked back at me and placed a finger on the side of her nose. I did the same and swallowed hard as the tears started flowing again.

THIRTEEN

The Standoff

I knew DCF was aware of Janine's admission. At both Clara Barton and Thoreau, the medical staff had called the emergency social worker on the overnight shift to get permission to treat. But I wanted them to hear it from me. So in the morning, I called Rhonda to personally tell her what had been going on.

"I don't think Janine is safe to live in the community," she informed me.

"What does that mean?" I asked.

"I'll be recommending she go back to Clinton Care."

My heart stopped. Clinton Care. Where Janine had languished for almost two years not getting well. Where they didn't specialize in eating disorders. Where she barely got an education in their therapeutic school.

Massachusetts Department of Children and Families was in the news a lot at that time. Three children in state custody had recently died, one right after the other. This led to renewed scrutiny of a beleaguered department and a new mandate from our governor. Whereas previously DCF's goals were two-pronged—to keep kids safe and keep families together—the goal now was singular: keep kids safe. And here was Janine, a child in state custody coming perilously close to losing her life.

I understood that the department had a low tolerance for risk at this time and that, from their perspective, Janine would be safer in an institution. From ours, she belonged with us. At home with people who loved her.

There was no point in arguing with Rhonda at that moment. I listened to all her reasons for making the astounding recommendation for re-institutionalization and I didn't argue. For now, I would just support Janine and advocate for her to come home when we were closer to her discharge date. She needed treatment, of course. A higher level of care than IOP. We would do residential. Partial. Anything but Clinton Care.

I tried to tell Janine's therapist on the general ward that she really needed to be transferred over to Alcott. No one was watching her eat here. No one was coaching her through meals. No one knew how. She could easily hide food and not eat.

At first, they insisted that they knew how to manage anorexics. They assured me they were on top of everything. I could see in her gaunt face and sunken cheeks that we were quickly losing all the ground we'd gained at IOP.

I asked them to weigh her.

They acquiesced.

She'd lost four pounds.

The first time Saul and I saw Janine with a feeding tube up her nose, the capped end taped to the side of her face, was simultaneously deeply disturbing and profoundly comforting. I did not want my child to require that thing. But she was getting much-needed nutrition, even if it was against her will.

Alcott treated both children and adults with anorexia. It was disheartening to look at these forty-year-old women still struggling to feed themselves. To think that Janine might need me decades from now to still feed her was deeply depressing. Some of the patients were so skeletal I wondered why they weren't in an ICU. Janine had balked at being transferred there. I thought it was because she could get away with not eating at Thoreau and I said so.

"You just don't get it, do you?" she asked me, a deep fatigue in her voice.

"I guess I don't," I answered. "What do you mean?"

Janine hesitated.

"My eating disorder makes me very competitive," she muttered, head down.

I looked at the girls on the ward with their waxy, gaunt skin, their hollow, blank stares. Most of them had feeding tubes, too. They played with them like jewelry accessories or hair extensions, twirling them around their fingers or flipping them over their ears. They seemed proud of them.

"You mean you want to be like them?" I asked, aghast that my daughter would strive for bones.

She nodded her head, looking ashamed. It was a dizzyingly honest and brave admission. A frightening window into her awful disease.

Part of me briefly wondered whether Rhonda was right. I hated to admit it, even for a split second. Janine had been in therapy and treatment for years and years. She knew every distress tolerance skill in the book. But in the moment—at the depth of her depression and height of her angst—she never seemed to be able to access any of it. She just acted out. Ran away from home. Jumped out of cars. Rhonda noted her "escalating behaviors" as a reason to send her back to Clinton Care. How could I disagree?

But I did disagree. Janine, more than anything, needed a family to help her and stand by her. She hadn't had that in so long. A doctor by the name of Bessel van der Kolk wrote a book called *The Body Keeps the Score* about childhood trauma. I saw him speak once at a conference. There, he'd asserted, "As soon as you take a child with a trauma history away from her family, she immediately starts to disintegrate." I could see in Janine that this was true. She was disintegrating before our eyes.

One night during visiting hours, Saul and Janine and I were playing a game called Head Bandz from the shelf of games on the ward. One player had a word taped to their forehead and had to guess that word based on clues given by the other players. We were laughing uproariously. It felt good. There was so little laughter in our lives these days.

As visiting hours were coming to an end, Janine asked us when she would be getting discharged.

"I just want to come home," she told us dejectedly.

We hesitated.

"Rhonda wants you to go back to Clinton Care," Saul finally told her.

"No!" she cried. "I can't go back there!"

Saul pulled Janine to his chest and kissed the top of her head.

"She says your behaviors are escalating. She thinks because you jumped out of Carolyn's car, you're not safe."

Saul paused, looking at me.

"And she thinks because you accused us of abuse, that *we're* not safe either."

Janine sat up, drying her eyes.

"I never meant for that to happen to you guys. You know that," she protested again.

I looked down at my lap. It was an old argument. The 51-A was still an open case with DCF and an open wound for me.

"And I never meant to scare you with the car thing either," she said craning her neck to try to look me in the eye. "You have to believe me. I'm really sorry."

Saul continued, "If you don't want to go back to Clinton Care, you have to start advocating for yourself. Tell people what you want, where you want to go."

Janine scoffed.

"No one ever listens to me."

"Oh yes, they do," Saul said, citing the 51-A for starters. "And whether you're using your words or not, you're telling them something."

Janine looked confused. "What do you mean?"

"You're telling them things with your behavior. Telling them you're not safe, maybe. Or that you need more help than we can give you."

"That's not true," Janine objected. "You guys are *just* what I need. You help me more than Clinton Care. More than Whitman. Definitely more than stupid DCF."

"Then start using your words and tell them that," I said. "Your therapists here. DCF. Advocate for yourself. Saul and I can only do so much, you know. They need to hear it from you."

I paused.

"You have more power than you think."

A staff member announced that visiting hours were over. We

hugged Janine in a sandwich hug. Gave her a sandwich kiss, one planted by each of us on each cheek.

"Love you," we said.

"Love you, too," she replied.

The heavy locked door clanged shut behind us. I turned and peered through the tiny glass window, wires crosshatching through the thick pane. I watched Janine pad down the hall toward her room. I laid a finger aside my nose, then turned and headed toward the elevator.

Rhonda and Dottie continued to push for Clinton Care as Janine's next placement. Whether they came in for the meetings (which they rarely did) or participated by conference call (their preferred modus operandi) their recommendation was always the same. Whitman wanted her to go to their own residential treatment program, "rezzy," as the kids called it. The staff who had been working with us in family counseling there could see that her relationship with us was very secure and attached. They knew she had spent more time at Clinton Care than anyone there had ever heard of and they agreed with us that she would not thrive there.

We were running out of time. Discharge day was fast approaching. Insurance companies only let patients stay in acute psychiatric care for so long. We decided to go over Rhonda's head and call the girls' lawyer, Theresa. Theresa had been a foster child herself, raised by an aunt under circumstances she did not share with us. She had been inspired to go into law and represent children like herself.

"DCF is supposed to tell me anytime there is a disruption in placement," she told us, indignant, her voice on speaker from Saul's cell phone on the coffee table. "No one from the department has told me about this. Let me make some calls and I'll get back to you."

Saul flipped his phone shut, satisfied.

"Theresa's on the case," he noted with confidence.

I worried that Rhonda would see this as questioning her authority, which I guess it was. Or at least disagreeing with her decisions. I worried she'd take out her anger with us on Janine and dig her heels in deeper. Or worse, recommend that the investigators support the 51-A that was still hanging over our heads. Take Janine away from us permanently.

I knew Clinton Care was just wrong for Janine. They never had an endpoint for her. No discharge goal to shoot for. We had a saying when I was in medical school. "No reason to admit, no reason to discharge." It was another way of saying that the team caring for patients needed to have clear goals in mind. Parameters that must be met before the patient could be sent home. Oxygen saturation above 95 percent on room air, say. Or able to keep down oral fluids for six hours without vomiting. It seemed to me that Rhonda's goal for Janine was to lock her up until she turned 18.

The day after our phone call to Theresa, I put in calls to Janine's therapist at Whitman as well as her dietician and her doctor. No one had called me back by noontime. I became paranoid. I convinced myself that Rhonda had instructed everyone there not to talk to me. Instead the opposite happened. That afternoon, they called me and put me on speaker phone for a conference call. They told me that Rhonda had agreed to switch Janine's insurance to Network Health so that they could transfer her to Whitman's residential program, what Saul and I and the staff at Alcott had been advocating for all along.

I wondered what had brought about the change, but I was afraid to ask. Had Rhonda asked herself what was wrong with this picture? That every one of Janine's clinicians as well as her foster parents thought she should not be in Clinton Care? That she was essentially going against medical advice by insisting on it? Or maybe Theresa had gotten to her. I didn't really care. All I knew was that we were back on track. Janine would be staying in the Whitman system, getting the help she needed from the system that had a proven track record with her.

Janine spent Halloween in the hospital and Thanksgiving in residential, so by the time Christmas was approaching, she was gaining weight, feeling healthier, and coming home on passes more frequently. The holiday tradition in the girls' family was a Yankee swap. Grandparents, aunts, uncles, cousins—second and first—all gathered together for a big potluck dinner. Everyone brought their specialties: hot crabbies, sloppy Joes in crock pots, peanut butter cookies topped with Hershey kisses. Afterward, gifts were passed around and traded in a rollicking, high energy, and, in some cases, beer-fueled spectacle. Janine and I had brought two gift-wrapped crocheted white hats, started together on our first pass home.

Janine's weight had plateaued at 94.8, seemingly stuck. Despite her goal weight being 103, set by Whitman (and four pounds higher than any goal weight set by Clinton Care), Janine vowed constantly never to get above 95.

"I'll let myself get to 95 pounds," she'd warn everyone. "But that's it."

Staff didn't argue at that point, planning to cross the 95-pound bridge when we got to it. In the meantime, hovering so close to her self-imposed goal weight was stressful.

I feared Janine wouldn't partake of any of her family's potluck, so I packed a frozen dinner for her along with a carton of 1 percent milk to take to the swap. I added a package of peanut butter crackers and juice for snack on the ride home.

We pulled up to her Auntie Kay's house in the late afternoon. It was a fancy home in a swanky suburb on Boston's South Shore. Laughter and music seeped through the wreathed front door as we approached. The sun was already beginning to set.

I smiled at Janine.

She looked terrified.

We rang the bell. The door swung open immediately as if it had a doorman on the other side.

"Come in!" Janine's uncle boomed. "Gimme your coats. What do you want to drink?"

We piled in, handing over our coats and putting in drink orders, as instructed.

We'd met most of the girls' family on various occasions: weddings, showers, graduations. They all greeted us now.

"Saul! Carolyn! Come in! Grab something to eat!"

They ooh'ed and ahh'ed over Janine. They hugged her and told her how good she looked. Asked about her life. But there seemed to be an awkwardness in their exchanges. Lots of kids only saw their aunts and uncles once a year at Christmas, I supposed. Most probably didn't have their foster parents in tow.

Saul filled a plate for himself and he and Janine found a spot on a bench in the corner of the kitchen. I heated Janine's dinner in the microwave oven and poked a straw into her milk carton.

"I'm not eating that!" she yelled when I laid her dish before her. "I've never eaten that before!" She wasn't even trying to keep her voice down. Heads turned.

"It's just like the ones you've eaten many times at the program," I assured her calmly and quietly.

"It's not measured! I'm not eating it!" She gave the plastic tray a tiny shove across the table. Conversations continued as eyes surreptitiously darted our way. Janine was oblivious.

"I've never eaten it! It's a new food! I don't eat new foods!" Janine continued to insist at top decibels. She seemed not to notice or mind that her voice was raised over the murmur of the crowd and the holiday music. I continued coaching in a soft voice, hoping hers would soon mirror mine.

"You always say you like that I cook ethnic foods. These foods are ethnic," I tried.

"I hate it!" she contradicted. "And I'm not drinking that milk. It's 140 calories."

"What's your little cousin's name?" I asked, trying a different tack. "The one in the red velvet dress over there?"

"Mindy," Janine muttered, voice finally lowered.

"Let's finish up here. Then we can go over and you can introduce me again. I'm sure she won't remember me from that one time we met."

"You always try to guilt me into eating! That's all you ever do!" she shouted.

This went on for the entire protocol-dictated thirty minutes of coaching. Her family was avoiding our corner of the kitchen like we were radioactive. At this Yankee swap, no one would swap places with us. Finally I took the now-cold dinner and threw it in the trash, then dumped the undrunk milk down the drain. I saw Saul continuing to talk to Janine on the bench. The crowd was too thick for me to get back to them. So I made small talk with some of the girls' family and picked at meatballs on toothpicks and cheese and crackers. I eventually squeezed my way back to the bench.

"What else do they have to eat here?" Janine asked me.

"I can ask Auntie Kay what they have to make a sandwich with, if you like."

Janine nodded.

"Can you fix me a plate?"

"Sure," I smiled.

I found some turkey in the fridge. I spread mayonnaise on two slices of white bread and laid a lettuce leaf on top of the meat before cutting the sandwich into two triangles. I added some raw veggies and a spoonful of dip. The only milk was skim, but beggars couldn't be choosers.

She ate the raw broccoli and carrots (no dip), then removed one of the three slices of turkey, laying it carefully to the side of her plate. She opened the sandwich, then closed it, then opened it again. She ate the lettuce leaf next, then tore the turkey slices into bite-sized pieces and ate them. She then nibbled at the bread, ultimately leaving a quarter of a slice on her plate. She drained her milk, then rose from the table and, zombie-like, headed into the crowd. Her behavior was back to the day we first brought her home on pass, unpacking her sandwich and shredding its contents. Considering her initial refusal, we were not displeased.

"What did you say to get her to eat?" Saul asked me.

"Me? I thought it was you. You were the one sitting with her."

Saul shook his head.

"It's just our brave girl," I said, leaning my head on his shoulder.

On the way home, I let Janine sit in front so she could play her music. At 9 o'clock I handed her the peanut butter crackers and juice I'd brought for snack.

She started to refuse.

I started to coach.

Finally, she unsnapped her seat belt and climbed into the back with me, her head in my lap.

"I'm fat," she sobbed. "I was the fattest one there. Everybody hates me. I'm a social idiot."

"No, you're not. You're brave and you're strong and I love you."

She wiped her running nose on her sleeve and ate her snack.

———

On Janine's next weigh-in day, she had lost 0.2 pounds.

I felt guilty. On the weekend pass, we had gone into Boston, spending hours slowly meandering down the spiral ramps of the New England Aquarium, then walking through Chinatown, buying fish for the new fish tank.

"We shouldn't have walked so much yesterday," I said.

"Oh, it's not that," Janine said, a little too brightly. "I exercise in my room every chance I get."

Was she happy to stay in residential? Was she sabotaging her own discharge? I couldn't tell. We'd been dealing with the compulsive exercise issue for months in family therapy. We searched for solutions and strategized, but there wasn't much Saul or I could do. We couldn't take her bedroom door off its hinges just to keep an eye on her. She was a teenage girl who needed her privacy. She had agreed to come and tell me when the urges to exercise struck. She never did. I promised to take a slow walk around the block with her to ward them off but she never took me up on my offer. Ultimately, this one was on her.

The next few passes home didn't go well. One weekend day after Christmas, Janine and I un-decorated the tree, carefully wrapping ornaments in newspaper and returning them to their cardboard boxes. Saul dragged the empty tree to the curb, scattering pine needles across the living room floor. While Saul vacuumed them up, Janine and I tucked the boxed decorations back in their storage place in the cellar.

As Janine and I sat at the kitchen counter after snack, she pulled out an emery board and began furiously filing her nails.

"Is something wrong?" I asked her.

A shoulder shrug. Then file file file.

"I can't help you if you don't tell me what's wrong, you know."

No shrug. Just file file file.

I waited patiently in silence. Finally, Janine laid down the emery board.

"I always get my hopes up for these weekend passes. I fantasize about how great they'll be." She twirled the emery board in little circles on the counter. "And then I'm just bored."

Saul offered to take her driving in New Hampshire. Janine didn't have her license, or even her learner's permit. Through a little Googling, she had discovered—and we had confirmed with our own online search—that 15-year-olds with no permit could drive in our bordering state with a grown-up and a birth certificate. She and Saul had spent countless hours driving the backroads and rolling hills of rural New Hampshire, Saul instructing her on the finer aspects of car driving.

She didn't want to drive today. That was apparently already getting old. I offered to take her to the pet store to buy new fish for our new Christmas aquarium and pat the chinchillas, something she always liked to do. Not today.

"Want to go on a nature walk?"

"No."

"Want to go to Jo-Ann Fabrics and find a crotchet project to do together?"

"No."

"I could help you study for your learner's permit."

Eye roll.

"How about getting our nails done together? My treat."

Janine shrugged. After a few moments, she called the salon and made an appointment. For 5:30.

"That's dinner time, Janine."

"Well, I'm bored."

"Well, dinner's almost ready. Why don't you call them back and postpone it until like seven?"

"Because I'm bored *now!*" Janine shouted.

Too quickly, I let myself get sucked into the drama.

"It's not a national emergency just because you're bored," I told her sarcastically, immaturely.

"Oh yes, it is!" she responded. "I'm trying to keep the urges to exercise away!"

With that, she ran upstairs and slammed her bedroom door. I knew what was happening. She planned to show me just how much of an emergency it was.

I ran upstairs after her and tried opening her door. It didn't budge. She must have been leaning against it.

"C'mon, Janine. Let me in," I coaxed.

"Fine," she said, letting the door fly open. "I'll just exercise right here in front of you."

With that, she got down on her rug and started doing slow sit-ups.

"One. Two. Three," a breathy exhalation with each number counted.

It was a heart-rending reveal. It felt voyeuristic and sad, watching her do something she'd been hiding from us for months.

I crouched down on the floor next to her.

"Janine, please," I said softly. "Stop that."

"Four. Five. Six."

I sat down and gently touched her elbow.

"C'mon. Get up. You've made your point. Let's go down and have dinner. Then we'll go to the salon."

"Let go of me!" Janine screamed, even though I wasn't holding her.

She sprang to her feet and ran out of the room. She went into the bathroom and slammed the door shut.

"I'm exercising. Now leave me alone," she huffed.

Again, I squeezed myself into the room.

"Oh Janine," I murmured, sadly shaking my head as she lay down on the cold bare tiles and resumed her crunches. It was one thing to watch your child starve herself. But I had never witnessed her desperate attempts to rid herself of the calories she took in.

I stood behind her so she could not lie down to complete her sit-up.

"Get off me, you psycho!" she screamed. "Don't touch me!"

"Janine, I'm just standing here."

Her sister's screams brought Mariah into the tiny bathroom. I was glad she was there this time so she could see that despite her sister's insistence that I get off her, I was actually standing innocently behind her, my hands to myself. We had been down that road before. I didn't want to go there again.

Mariah made a rapid assessment of the situation.

"Nope," she shook her head. "This is not happening."

She stepped in between me and her sister and wrapped her arms around Janine's chest and dragged her to her feet. Janine, like a squirming toddler, lifted her arms straight up in the air, trying to slip from Mariah's grip. Mariah just held on tighter.

"Nope. That's not happening either," she said.

I left the room. Mariah could be tough with Janine in a way that I couldn't. My approach, in general, was usually one of quiet support, while Mariah was free to tell it like it was. Or at least how she saw it. And I certainly couldn't lay my hands on her in this state. That much was very clear. The 51-A filed on us had not yet been decided. We didn't need another. I decided to let Mariah use her tough love. I left the bathroom, lingering in the hall on the other side of the closed door.

"Do you want to die?" I could her Mariah screaming at Janine. "Is that what you want? To be dead in the ground like Dad?! 'Cause that's what's going to happen if you keep up like this!"

I winced at her harsh words. I heard no response from Janine. Both girls soon emerged somber and retreated to their respective rooms.

We ate as a family. No one spoke. After dinner, Saul and I sat on the couch to watch the evening news. Janine came downstairs with her arms loaded with clothes to bring back to Whitman. She put the pile on the coffee table, then sat between us and started sobbing.

"I hate what I'm turning into," she wailed, laying her head in my lap and throwing her feet onto Saul's.

"You're not turning into anything," Saul assured her, massaging her feet.

"Mariah called me a monster," she cried. I played with her hair like she liked me to.

"Mariah is just worried about you. She's scared and frustrated," I said.

"We all do things we're not proud of," Saul went on. "You can't focus on one word someone says in the heat of the moment."

As distressed as Janine was, part of me was glad that she was ashamed of her behavior. It had taken an extreme statement that only her sister could make to trigger that insight, to cause her to see how she was manipulating the whole family.

And, as always, I'm sure this was also testing us. By showing us the exercise urges that torment her, by slamming doors and calling us names, she was really asking, *How ugly can my behavior get before it's unacceptable and I'm asked to leave? Can I make these people un-love me by being wretched enough?*

In just a few months' time, Janine would host a Saint Patrick's Day party at our house that would get out of control. Although we had okayed the initial guest list, eventually uninvited partygoers showed up and were under-age drinking. Saul and I had to ask them to leave. They did, but they also left a mess, which a couple of Janine's friends stayed to help her clean up.

The next morning, the first question to me and Saul would be "Do I still get to live here?" I would remember the colored-paper collage on Ben's wall of all the obstacles Janine had overcome and her magic-markered words about always worrying she would inadvertently do something wrong in a foster home and be asked to leave.

Now, we said a lot of "I love you's" and gave lots of hugs and reassurances that we weren't going anywhere.

"You're quite stuck with us whether you like it or not," Saul teased, rubbing her head with his knuckles in a gentle noogie.

My own reassurances felt far less resolute than Saul's, my resolve still shaken by the 51-A. I kept quiet, letting Saul take the lead on this one. I knew in my head that we weren't going anywhere. We would be her last foster home. We were the last stop on the struggle bus for both of these girls. I knew this in my head. I just needed to feel it again in my heart.

FOURTEEN

Living in the Slipstream

Janine was discharged from residential treatment straight to IOP when she reached 95.8 pounds, skipping the partial program altogether. At last, she could return to Newburyport High. We had a re-entry meeting with the school, required after a student had been out for a significant amount of time. We had done it with Neil after his traumatic brain injury and Mariah after her suspension. Now it was Janine's turn.

Her teachers knew about her eating disorder, her depression and her social anxiety. They did their best to ease her back into school and teenage life. They let her do a couple of half-days at first, allowing her to work her way up to full-time. They also let her skip mid-term exams on a medical exemption, requiring her to make up only critical work, then allowing her grades to stand as they had been when she was first hospitalized.

Janine was a smart girl. She would catch up academically. The social piece was much more of an obstacle for her. Suddenly, she was the awkward new kid all over again. Plus, with her three after-school days taken up in treatment, there was even less time to hang out with old friends or make new ones.

"I have no friends!" she'd wail. "Nobody likes me!"

I understood her fears and frustrations, but her claims ran counter to the interactions I'd observed. In the alt room, at theater classes, in our home.

"You always seem to have friends to me," I said. "You're chatty and social. It looks to me like the other kids gravitate to you. You're a natural leader."

"Yeah, well, that's just 'cause you're there," she said. I thought she meant that she went into people-pleasing mode when I was around, only pretending to be social. Then she went on. "You're my back-up," she explained. "With you around, I have more confidence."

I smiled. It made me feel good on one level. Needed. Useful. That I was doing something right, that I was appreciated, that I was good at fostering. Feelings that were few and far between these days. It also re-confirmed Janine's deep lack of self-confidence.

Janine struggled with the relatively looser structure of IOP compared with residential. She tried using behaviors again, tearing her wraps into tiny pieces and pushing them around on her plate to avoid eating. At her first weigh-in, she weighed 95.4, almost half a pound less than her discharge weight. This did not surprise me. Janine had refused or restricted during her first two dinners home. We had a meeting with staff at which we all signed a contract saying that if Janine went more than six hours without eating or drinking, we were to take her to the emergency room for hydration with IV fluids and labs. Janine was somber but agreed. She knew everyone in the room was trying to help her. She still struggled so much with helping herself.

One day, in therapy, she read me a letter she had written to her eating disorder. In it, she wisely observed that Edie was not her friend.

"Friends don't try to make you feel bad about yourself," she noted. "Or call you fat, or shame you just for feeding your body."

I was proud of her and told her so. She smiled and tucked the letter into her purse.

"I'm going to carry it with me all the time so I can re-read it when I'm struggling."

The next time she felt the urge to restrict, I gently reminded her of the letter she'd written. She stormed upstairs, came down with her purse, took out the letter and tore it into tiny pieces and threw them in my face.

When I brought up the whole incident in our next family therapy session, I was in tears.

"It seemed like she was making such progress," I said.

Joanne nodded very matter-of-factly.

"Yup," she said with a knowing smile. "She'll probably write ten more letters and rip them up ten more times."

Fourteen. *Living in the Slipstream*

At first, it comforted me to know that this up and down trajectory of progress in eating disorder was normal. In fact, in one group session, Joanne drew an X and Y axis on a white board in the front of the room. She labeled the X axis recovery and the Y axis time. Then she drew a neat line from the X/Y intersection straight up and to the right, dividing the graph into two perfectly symmetrical halves.

"Is this what recovery looks like?" she asked the girls.

They responded with a resounding *"Nooo!"* in unison.

"Who wants to show us what recovery *really* looks like?" she asked, proffering her marker to the group.

Before anyone else could respond, Janine jumped up and grabbed the pen from Joanne, then proceeded to etch out the most twisted back and forth and up and down and left and right journey imaginable with her marker. The more she drew, the more her audience howled, heads nodding in agreement with Janine's depiction. They stomped their feet on the floor and pounded the table in laughter. "Yeah!" they cried, pointing to Janine's messy graph.

Ultimately, though, as more and more time went on in therapy, this crazy up and down trajectory became discouraging. Progress was so elusive. It was hard to patiently coach Janine and try to tolerate her vicious backlash against us simply for trying to feed her. The stress of ten-plus hours a week in treatment kept my stomach in a perpetual knot of anxiety. Much of the time these days, it felt like I could throw up at any time.

It was so hard to stay in the moment. To avoid all the what-ifs. I always assumed mealtimes would end in disaster. I had done it that very night. I had made coconut rice as a side dish for family dinner. As I was packing it up, the fears started.

Janine is never going to eat this.

Maybe I should just serve her half a cup instead of a whole one.

Maybe I should cook another grain and bring it as a back-up.

As it turned out, she ate the whole cup without a word. I needed to trust that maybe this program had the answers. That maybe the solution was not in the past or the future but in the right now.

Still, some days I felt like I had nothing left to give. Mariah was living with her boyfriend Marcus and skipping a lot of her high school classes. I got notices in the mail that she was failing and might not graduate. Janine texted me regularly, crying that she was a social pariah and complaining about the dressing on her salad.

One night in family therapy in IOP, we set a goal for Janine to initiate one social interaction that week. We also set a positive consequence for meals completed. If she could be 100 percent for the rest of the week, we would all go to the movies together. Then we talked about negative consequences.

"Well, you're not taking my phone away again," she said snarkily. "We all remember how *that* ended."

I couldn't believe she was smirking over something that was so devastating for me. At that point, we still did not even have a verdict in the 51-A that had been filed against us when she claimed to be too afraid to come home.

"Oh, and I'm already going to the movies with Liz this week, so you can't take that away either."

At dinner, Janine refused her meal as well as her Boost. Sometimes I thought she took a perverse pride in being the most difficult client there.

It was January 15. The eve of the anniversary of her father's death. I knew these markers were hard for her. After all, she'd jumped out of my car the night before her mother's birthday.

One of the social workers, Michael, sat down with us. Michael was a fill-in from the Waltham partial program. We had never met him before.

"You know you *can* take her phone away," he told us matter-of-factly. "And she does not *have* to go to the movies with Liz."

If Janine heard him, she showed no sign. As for me, I bit my lip and tried not to cry. I felt like I was being accused yet again of failing. I spent a lot of my time at IOP trying not to cry.

"Your call," Michael shrugged casually as he walked away from our table. "Unless you do something, she will always be in charge."

I didn't know who he meant by "she," Janine or her eating disorder. It almost didn't matter. Who was *not* in charge was clearly me.

A part of me felt that Michael didn't know us. We had special circumstances. Didn't we? We were foster parents. We couldn't say or do things bio parents could. I couldn't take her by the shoulders and shake her or turn her head to look at me, as the 51-A had demonstrated so spectacularly. I also worried about how hard to push someone with such a trauma background as Janine's. I was still embarrassed and ashamed that I had to be called out like that by someone who'd just met me for the first time. It was as if he could tell I was a failure just by looking at me. Like I radiated disaster and disappointment.

That night, I lay in my bed sobbing. I had not felt this low since we'd started on this journey. Earlier that day, I'd cleaned my desk, finding a jackknife under the clutter. I'd cleaned my nails with it. Now all I could think of was *I know exactly where that jackknife is. I can find it in the dark.*

I got up and went downstairs, got a drink of water and sat on the couch. The knife was just a fleeting thought. I couldn't desert my family. My boys were grown but they still needed a mother. I couldn't leave Saul alone with the girls. Couldn't be one more person who abandoned Mariah and Janine. But for that split second, the thought of not having to wake up and face all this in the morning was a cold comfort. For one minute I could relate to Janine's suicidality, just wanting everything to go away.

The next morning, after I'd had time to let Michael's words gel, I realized he was right. I *could* be firmer with Janine. I could make consequences and stick to them. Instead of feeling weakened and ashamed and a failure, I felt empowered. It had taken me getting to my complete breaking point, my utter humiliation, my personal rock-bottom, to get me to the place where I knew what I had to do.

I always tell parents of willful toddlers in my practice that their children need discipline. That it is scary for a two-year-old to think there is no one in charge but him. That he or she can do anything they want with no consequence. They may not act like it, but they really do want their parents to step up and lay down some rules. I give this talk almost every day at work. And yet I had needed someone else to teach me the same lesson with my own child.

Janine was coming to work with me that day, having no school due to a teacher training. At breakfast, Janine was not just refusing her oatmeal. She was peeling off her fingernails and dumping them into the cereal so I couldn't make her eat it. Saul and I laid out our new resolve.

"Your plans to go to the movies with Liz *are* in fact on the table, Janine, and *will* be cancelled if you don't drink your Boost," Saul told her.

"That's cool," Janine said, pushing her Boost side by side with her ruined breakfast.

"And we *will* take your phone away if you continue to restrict today," he added.

Janine pretended to choke on her own saliva, doing a little animated spit-take.

"Even after what I did last time?"

Saul and I had already discussed this.

"I'll just call Sprint and turn off your data," he explained. "You'll physically have your phone, but it will be useless."

She didn't say a word. I could almost see the wheels turning in her head as she was confronted by this newly emboldened parental front.

I had packed her a tuna fish sandwich, some cherry tomatoes and a carton of milk for lunch. While I saw my morning patients, Janine helped out by running old bills and office papers through the shredder, all the while pointedly ignoring me.

When it came time for lunch, instead of eating with me, Janine crawled under my partner's desk with her phone. After the requisite 30 minutes had elapsed, I re-wrapped her sandwich and put it back in the fridge. I opened a bottle of Boost and placed it on the desk. She got up and knocked it to the floor. I called Saul and told him to have Sprint turn off Janine's phone, purposely not texting him so she could hear what we were doing.

She stormed out of the office.

I did not follow her.

We were in Hillsboro, her hometown. The town where she grew up in a condo within walking distance of my office. Not the one she'd been removed from, but the first one her family had owned. She'd shown it to me once on our way to work.

"We had a pool," she'd told me wistfully.

Also within walking distance was St. John the Baptist Church where she'd attended mass as a kid. Where her father's funeral had taken place. Mamie Mary, an old family friend who was like another grandmother to the girls, lived nearby.

I wasn't worried that she wouldn't return, but I did let DCF know what was going on.

"Call the police," her social worker told me.

I did not call the police.

Sure enough, about a half hour later, Janine returned, on her phone. The data cancellation, we would learn, sometimes took a while to kick in.

"They're taking my phone away, Liz," she was sobbing. "And I can't go to the movies with you."

A pause.

"I *can't* just eat, Liz. You don't understand. Carolyn gave me *way* too much tuna fish."

Another pause.

"I don't *want* to get better. All I want is my eating disorder. That's all I want in the whole entire world." She was bawling tearlessly now.

As I listened to her, my heart did not break or even crack like it usually did. Hearing her litany of complaints made me realize that it was eating disorder we were listening to. Edie was angry at being challenged. Edie felt trapped and that meant we could win. That we were, in fact, winning.

When Janine got off the phone, I re-opened the sandwich I had wrapped up and stuck in the fridge. I set out the unopened milk for her on my partner's desk.

"Saul's coming to get you and take you home, so you don't have to stay here for the whole day," I told her, rubbing her shoulders. She nodded and sniffed. Then she picked up her sandwich and took the first bite.

The old adage "one step forward, two steps back" didn't even come close to describing the twists and turns through recovery that Janine's marker had so dramatically captured on that white board in

IOP. One of the mothers in the family support group offered an apt description.

"It's like one of those giant ocean liners trying to correct its course," she said, describing her daughter's journey. "It's hard to change direction with so much momentum behind you. And any movement that is eked out is barely noticeable at all."

"Like the *Titanic*," another parent noted with grim humor.

"I hope not," I said quietly, almost to myself, though I did feel like we were living in eating disorder's slipstream.

With our new No-More-Mr.-and-Mrs.-Nice-Guy approach, I felt we were on the right track. Eating disorder was pushing back with spewed insults and fingernails in cereal. But Janine, our Janine, was fighting through.

One day, Saul was again making the family favorite for breakfast: oatmeal. Into ours he dumped blueberries and poured maple syrup. Into Janine's went the requisite fat—slivered almonds—along with the berries.

"Wait," she said suddenly with a smile. "Can maple syrup count as my fat? I love maple syrup."

I hesitated. This was so unusual for Janine. To admit that she liked a certain food was rare. To ask for it, rarer still. At that point she was back on her meal plan and her meal plan required a fat.

"Well, maple syrup isn't a fat," I broached. "But you can certainly have as much of it as you want."

Janine looked dejected.

"No, that's okay," she said glumly.

Still, it was a small breakthrough. And every little victory had to be celebrated. Janine had asked for food. For so long, the ugly voice in her head had been telling her she didn't deserve to eat. Like that sad little girl in Harriet Brown's bakery, her nose pressed to the glass.

Janine made progress in the area of body image as well. For the first time in almost two years, she handed me a pair of size 00 jeans and a pair of scissors.

"Just cut them up," she ordered with a wave of her hand as if to make it happen. This was something the program had long advised, but Janine had resisted. She then aggressively took those same scissors to her favorite leggings, assuring that she wouldn't be tempted to diet her way back into them. For the first time in forever, she was looking toward the future with hope and determination.

Janine was discharged from IOP in March. It freed up ten hours a week of after-school time for all of us. For me, it meant not having to plan, cook and pack three evening meals and not driving four hours a week. For Janine, it meant spending more time with her friends. It also meant she was often on her own with those friends. I wasn't supervising after-school snacks on some days. Some evenings she wanted to eat out with her friends.

Though eating disorder was a very skillful liar, I still had a hard time believing that Janine was eating all these meals and snacks she claimed to be when she was out. Even when she took pictures of food with her cell phone and texted them to me at my request, I had my doubts.

At our next weigh-in at Children's Hospital, my doubts were confirmed. Janine was down two pounds from her discharge weight.

"Why do you think that is, Janine?" the nutritionist asked her.

Janine (meaning eating disorder) was like a caged criminal, eyes darting, fingers pulling at her hair.

"I exercise in my room constantly," she started. "I do like a hundred crunches a day."

I just shook my head at Edie's lie. It was so obvious to me that what she was really saying was *Please don't increase my meal plan. Don't make me eat more food.*

"You haven't been eating with your friends when you said you were, have you?" I asked.

Janine stared silently at her lap.

"No mozzarella sticks at Friendly's with Emma. No power bar at Richdale's. No popcorn at Becca's."

Janine shook her head. It saddened me to realize that, as far as she had come, she was still unable to feed herself.

We made a plan with her nurse practitioner to go back to supervised meals and snacks at least until she had regained the two pounds she'd lost. Her nutritionist added that if she was walking a lot with her friends, she had to have a Boost instead of milk.

Body image issues, though better, still plagued Janine. Some days she had such a poor self-image, she refused to go to school or get out of bed. We tried to strategize with her therapist who suggested picking out an outfit the night before and having an "emergency back-up ensemble" selected: go-to clothes she felt comfortable wearing and looked good in. Some days, nothing worked. It got to be such a problem that DCF set us up with a home mentor, a clinician named Barb who came to the house twice a week for therapy sessions and who was available for times when Janine refused to go to school.

Refusal days were stressful and disruptive. There were ripple effects through the whole family and beyond. On days that I was off, Saul could leave for work while I continued coaching, encouraging, bribing Janine to attend school. If I had to work, Saul would ask one of the boys to cover the store for him. I often had to cancel my first few patients while I waited for Barb to arrive. I told Janine I couldn't keep cancelling or I'd have no practice left.

"Thanks for making me feel guilty if you lose your precious little practice," she told me petulantly.

Her clinicians helped her make a key ring with ten different stress levels written out on laminated cards with a corresponding distress-tolerance skill she could use to cope with each stressor.

I will squeeze a frozen orange.

I will practice opposite emotion.

I will pet my cats. All strategies she'd known for years.

We bought her a white board to put outside her room so that she could communicate with us without speaking when she felt shut down.

On many days, nothing worked. On those days, having Barb to call was a godsend. Soon I started leaving Janine alone and going to work, knowing Barb was on her way.

At her next weigh-in, Janine had reached 100 pounds. Her weight had never been in triple digits before. She'd developed the disorder when she was just thirteen and weighed 85 pounds. Her goal weight was at least 103 and she never agreed to reach it. She was visibly shaking when she got off the scale. This was huge.

I texted Saul just to give him a heads' up about Janine's huge accomplishment as well as her anxious reaction to it. Soon her phone sounded.

"Oh my God!" she squealed, checking her texts.

Saul had sent her a picture of a puppy and said, "I guess we need to start looking." Weighing over 100 pounds was such a tremendous objective that we had promised her a puppy if she got there. It had started on a Sunday night when Janine was having a hard time leaving us and going back to the program.

"If I reach my goal weight, can I get a puppy?" she had asked.

Saul and I had looked at each other and rolled our eyes. Our house was a zoo already. We had rescued the girls' two cats from a shelter. We had Homer. We had bought Janine an aquarium for Christmas. So what was one more animal if it served as an incentive to gain weight?

"We'll discuss it," I told her.

"Yay!" she said, jumping up and down.

"That doesn't mean yes!" I had warned as she and Saul got on their coats and headed out the door.

"Yes, it does!" she'd countered, skipping off to the car.

Now, even with a puppy in her future, eating remained hard. Janine started threatening to refuse the next meal or snack before she'd even finished the current one. When I sent her to school with a kale salad for a side, already dressed with homemade lemon vinaigrette, she texted me *Do NOT expect me to eat snack after school.* Perhaps it was just eating disorder's last gasp, because she always ate whatever she'd threatened to refuse.

For dinner one night I'd made a meatloaf, baked potatoes and oven-fried pickles, something I'd never had before the girls introduced me to them at Lexie's, the local hamburger joint. Janine made a face.

"That's two servings of grains."

I made a face back.

"A tablespoon of breadcrumbs is not a serving of grain."

Janine acquiesced with a little harrumph.

"Well, they're grain-*y*," she said in a backed-down kind of way.

The next night I made scampi. Again, Edie was not pleased.

With this weight. With this new, firmer parenting. With Janine giving in to eating. Our conversations sounded the same, but there was a resignation to them that gave me hope that Edie was on her last legs. There was none of the piss and vinegar of our old battles.

"Do you have to give me this much pasta?"

"Yes."

"This is way more than a cup."

"No, it's not."

"This is way more than I need."

"It is exactly what you need."

"I seriously cannot eat this much food."

"Just do your best."

"What if I don't?"

"You can drink Boost."

"No."

"Then just work on your shrimp."

Right before she picked up her fork and started eating came her new go-to line.

"Well, you can forget about me eating snack tonight."

With Janine getting better, healing, gaining weight, I began to be able to breathe again. In IOP, I had felt like the rat in the maze—except instead of chasing cheese, I was making it: choosing recipes, shopping for ingredients, preparing, packing, all the while following blindly an endless labyrinth.

But we had found our way out.

Led by Janine.

Breathing again meant not just feeling more confident in her ability to thrive, not just freeing up ten more hours a week. It also meant I had time to be something more than just an inferior eating disorder coach and a floundering foster mom. I had kept up my practice during this first year of foster care. Seeing patients throughout had given me a sense of competence and accomplishment. With Janine tentatively on her way to a normal teenage life, I could spend more of my time doing something else that I loved.

When my second child Neil (and I now thought of myself as having four children in my family) had suffered a traumatic brain injury, I had started volunteering for my local Brain Injury Association. I spoke at local civic organizations like Lions Clubs and Elks. I spoke at colleges during alcohol awareness week and to juniors and seniors before prom, reminding them all about the dangers of underage drinking and drunk driving. When my memoir came out about our experience with traumatic brain injury, I was invited to be the keynote speaker at many regional Brain Injury Association educational conferences. Even though it was my job to inspire my audiences, invariably it was they who inspired me. Survivors, family members, caregivers and health care workers all had their stories to tell. Speaking at these events was therapeutic for me. Just as part of Janine's recovery entailed reading her trauma narrative again and again, I also felt healed by telling my family's story and hearing about others' triumphs over obstacles.

I was preparing to give my biggest keynote address ever—nearly 1,000 audience members. The opening of my speech involved a reference to Viktor Frankl's book *Man's Search for Meaning*. Frankl was a neurologist and a psychiatrist and a survivor of the Holocaust. He wrote his book in just nine days after his release. When he was in the camps, he came to believe that the people who survived were the ones who were able to make goals. To see some purpose for their lives. To find some meaning in their suffering. He came to believe that the will to live was fed by purpose. That life was not primarily a quest for pleasure or power, but a search for meaning. He quoted Nietzsche who said, "He who has a *why* to live can bear almost any *how*."

As I worked on my speech, I thought about my own life. Frankl's point was that we cannot control how life treats us or what curveballs are thrown our way. We can, however, control how we respond. And in doing that, we find our meaning.

I had never been a person who believed that everything happened for a reason. There was no reason that Neil was hit by a drunk driver. No sense behind the loss of his girlfriend. It had simply happened. I had to try to impose meaning on those tragic random events myself. By writing. By volunteering. By speaking. I had come to believe deeply in the power of words. How sharing our stories helped us all.

The speech went well. As always, audience members who were too shy to ask questions at the microphone swarmed me afterward to share their stories. To tell me how their son or daughter or sister or brother was just like Neil. We hugged. We shed tears. We thanked each other for sharing our stories.

In the back of my mind, I was thinking of my girls. Mariah and Janine. How they were shaping this new chapter in my life. It wasn't easy. My friends were all enjoying their empty nests. Some were retiring. Over lunch I heard about their volunteer work and their vacations. Their children's weddings. The grandchildren. Me? I was hanging out in emergency rooms with concussed teenagers, bawling my eyes out for letting eating disorder run roughshod over me, and enduring verbal abuse from an illness that had invaded my child.

My friend Rachel, one day while I was relating my experiences over soup and half an egg salad sandwich, said, "Gee, it doesn't sound very enjoyable."

I bristled.

I didn't have an answer for her at the time. I think I stammered something like *Oh yes, it is.* On the way home, alone with my thoughts, I reflected on her words and my response. I realized that enjoyment wasn't the point. It wasn't about enjoyment. It wasn't about how happy I was. It was about fulfillment. Like Viktor Frankl's book maintained, it was about purpose.

I realized, giving my talk to a room full of survivors, that my life was full of meaning. Full of hard work, yes. Full of anger and frustration and sadness, too. But more than anything, it was full of love. As the girls left the house they'd call out to us, "Love you!" "Love you too!" we'd reply. Or sometimes it would be our shorthand "Mwah!" "Mwah!" blowing kisses. Or emojis—hearts and kisses in texts going back and forth. Oh yes. Our life was full of love.

I had found my why and for that I was grateful.

In Coda

FIFTEEN

A Rocky Road Gets Rockier

We did not learn of the outcome of the abuse and neglect investigation for two long months. There was no big meeting around a conference table. There was not even a phone call. Certainly not an apology.

The results came by mail: in a nondescript envelope like many we receive from the state. It could have been a clothing check. I opened it with shaking hands. It was a single page, a few short paragraphs. The allegations against both Saul and I had been unsupported.

I refolded the letter, placed it back in its envelope and filed it in the secretary in the hall alongside the titles for our cars and our home insurance policy. I stood looking at the closed drawer as if expecting it to pop back open with different results. That was it. The upshot of months of sleepless nights and churning guts would sit in that drawer, filed away like a gas receipt.

I thought I would feel more relief. I didn't expect to feel like doing back flips in the kitchen and I didn't. I just thought that after all we had been through, the anxiety and unease, the weight lifting off of me would have brought more of a liberated feeling.

It did not.

Maybe I'd just incorporated this sense of trepidation I'd had since the accusation first surfaced—*I'm afraid to go home* into my being. Maybe the terror that it could all happen again would never leave me. It would just feel normal now, a part of me. Like a scar. Or maybe it was because I knew that we were not abusive. We were not neglectful. We loved Janine and maybe deep inside I trusted DCF to know that, too.

Or maybe I was just exhausted.

In the spring of that year, Janine's eating disorder took a strange turn, one none of us saw coming or knew how to thwart. She started bingeing. She had never binged before and I frankly wouldn't have believed her ever capable. The first time it happened was after using marijuana one night. She told me in the morning that during the night she had eaten granola and milk, yogurt, peanut butter on toast, a Klondike bar, and an entire sleeve of Fig Newtons.

She was miserable. She refused to go to school, and given this new anomalous behavior, I knew there was no point in even trying to coax her there.

I called her therapist for advice. Rosie was very reassuring about this bizarre new aspect to Janine's illness.

"She's used food and eating as a coping mechanism for so long, it's not surprising that she's doing it now. Then, it was restricting. Now, it's bingeing. But it's all just Janine trying to cope."

She said the key was to try to figure out what stressors were triggering the bingeing behaviors. Janine had many. Her mother was sick—in a group home and on meds. Janine was having monthly supervised visits with her. They were very triggering. Linda would grab her stomach rolls and say to Janine, "Look how fat I am!" Or she would take out pictures of when she was younger and exclaim, "Look how thin I used to be!" Sometimes she would just dwell in the past. "It's all my fault you girls are in DCF custody." Some of her statements were true. Some were not. All were unhelpful.

High school had its stressors, too. She was finishing her first year of public school in almost three years and doing well academically despite her many setbacks and long absences. But girls could be cliquey. Feelings could get hurt.

"Me and Julia are fighting a lot lately," Janine shared with Rosie. I was proud of her for trying to identify the stressors that may be triggering her binges.

Rosie gave Janine strategies to avoid "emotional over-eating" as she preferred to call it.

"Always sit to eat," she told her. "People who binge tend to eat standing up or pacing. Just the simple act of sitting may relieve that urge."

"Keep a journal," she also suggested. "Ask yourself, 'What am I feeling right now? What am I thinking?' You can keep eating if you want to, but keep writing, too."

Janine agreed to all of it. It was a pattern we had seen for over a year. In therapy or at the doctor's office, she could identify issues, outline strategies. She had learned so many skills over the years to tolerate distress. Her problem was being incapable of accessing those skills in the moment.

Despite all the strategies Rosie suggested, Janine's bingeing became more frequent. She binged when I was at work, when I ran out to the grocery store, when I went to the bank to cash my check. I couldn't leave her alone.

I felt like a prisoner.

Sometimes the detritus in the sink gave her away. Bowls with rings of milk, dishes with dried ice cream, knives licked almost clean of peanut butter and cream cheese, melted then congealed butter on plates. Sometimes there was nothing to give it away, to the point where sometimes I wondered out loud if she had really binged or was just finding an excuse not to go to school or to restrict.

"When you eat cereal straight out of the box, there's nothing to show," she explained desolately.

Oh.

Our home looked like a prison, too. At Janine's request, we bought bicycle locks and wound them around cabinet pulls and fridge and freezer door handles. We later learned from her therapist that this was a misinformed and ineffective strategy.

"It makes the person crave whatever's locked up even more," she explained.

It was reassuring to me to hear Rosie discuss Janine's bingeing.

"It's just another part of the disease," she told Janine. "Your body has been starved for so long, it's finally had enough and is demanding to be fed. We see this all the time."

If they saw this all the time, then why hadn't we ever heard about this at Whitman? I wondered. I could guess why they didn't warn the patients themselves of this possibility. If these anorexic teenagers ever thought that once they started to recover they may start binge eating, they'd never try to get better at all.

But why not at least tip off us parents?

We tried everything we could think of to help Janine with this new behavior. We limited what snacks we bought, although she still needed the calories. We laid out a pen and paper on the counter for her to journal as Rosie had advised. I told her she could wake me up in the middle of the night and I would sit with her if that would help.

Nothing did.

Rosie told us that no matter what, Janine was not to restrict after a binge. She was not to purge either (something she had never done) nor compulsively exercise (something she continued to struggle with). Any of those three behaviors—restricting, purging or exercising amounted to the same thing, Janine trying to rid herself of the calories she'd just consumed—and each could lead to a new and unhealthy cycle.

It was all very overwhelming. It broke my heart to listen to her keen after a binge.

"Why is this happening to me?" she wailed. "What's wrong with me?"

I tried to reassure her using Rosie's words.

"It's part of your recovery. It means you can finally feed yourself. It's a good thing."

But seeing her in such pain made my own words ring hollow.

Worst of all, in all of this turmoil, Janine did not have her sister around. Just one month after she turned 18, Mariah moved into an apartment with her boyfriend. Janine was devastated. She used to tell me all the time how she and Mariah would someday share a place. They'd take a trip to Ireland, their shared homeland, then come back to the States and move in together.

Mariah was always very independent. She rarely asked for help with anything. She was a very go-it-alone sort of person, sometimes to a fault. Her response to the losses in her life was to buck up, grit her teeth, and say, "I don't need you. I can do this by myself. I got this."

I admired that about Mariah, even though I wished she'd lean on us a little or reach out more. As often as I told her she could ask us anything, she always kept her cards pretty close to the vest. In her senior year, when I learned that she had put a deposit down on a prom dress and was planning on making monthly payments on it until it was hers, I went down to the bridal shop where she'd gotten it and paid for it in full.

When Mariah went in to make her next payment and learned what I'd done, she was overwhelmed with gratitude.

"Why did you do that, Carolyn?" she asked me.

"Because you didn't ask," I said honestly.

She was a very hard worker. When she was focused, she got straight A's. She had always had a job since she was fifteen years old, earning her own way in the world. But she was eager to grow up and be on her own. Too eager, it seemed to me.

I knew that Mariah had the skills to live independently. She always set her own alarm, rarely oversleeping. She got herself to work on time and seldom missed a day. But I thought she was going too fast, making things harder on herself than they needed to be. I wanted her to stay with us, save some money. Think about college.

"Paying bills and keeping an apartment isn't all it's cracked up to be," I warned.

Still, I went to the meeting where Marcus and Mariah made their case to DCF. Marcus had found an apartment and was already living there. I suspected that on the nights Mariah told me she was staying at Desiree's or Felecia's that she was probably there too. The pair presented a budget and they seemed to have thought of everything. I vouched for both kids as hard workers and capable students.

"Do I think they can do this?" I asked DCF rhetorically. "Absolutely."

"Do I think they *should*?" I continued. "Not right now," I answered quietly. There were nods all around the table of social workers. I looked Mariah right in the eye.

"She can do it. I'll support her if she does do it. But I'd rather she stay home until she graduates."

Mariah met my gaze with a shy smile and a quiet "Thanks."

One way or another, Mariah was going to go it alone.

Janine began refusing to eat the entire next day after a nighttime binge. She tried to hide it. I came home one day to find her in the basement with Mariah and Marcus, taking turns swinging in a hammock hung from the big wooden beams in our ceiling. I asked her to come upstairs and have lunch with me.

"I already ate," she informed me.

"Oh? What did you eat?"

"A sandwich."

"What kind?"

"I don't know!" she shouted at me. "Whatever was in the fridge!"

I looked in the refrigerator then went back into the basement.

"All the deli meat is brand new. Unopened. You did not eat a sandwich at all," I told her calmly.

"Fine!" she barked. "I ate snacks for lunch. I lied about it 'cause I thought you'd be mad at me."

When I found no evidence of snack wrappers in the trash, she claimed she had thrown them away in the basement. When that was discovered to be a lie, she claimed to have eaten cereal right out of the box—hence no trash.

It had to be exhausting. I could almost see Janine's mind frantically altering her story—her lie—to accommodate whatever new truth I'd turned up. All to hide her restricting.

This was new behavior and it frightened me. When Janine first started bingeing, she was completely freaked out by it, sobbing, "Why is this happening?" Later, she was defiant, steadfastly refusing to eat after a binge. Now, she seemed to have reverted to her old anorexic ways. Starving herself then lying about it.

That night I had a troubled sleep. I dreamed Janine was hacking off body parts—arms, legs—in order to weigh less. I woke in a trembling sweat. I went downstairs to get a glass of water. When I turned on the kitchen light, I saw a note written by Janine on a napkin in Magic Marker. It read *"Please don't make me eat breakfast today. I got up and binged at 4 a.m."*

I looked at the clock.

It was two o'clock in the morning.

To me, this added another layer of scary to the deception. It was planned. Not just lying after the fact, but before it, too.

I emailed her doctor and her therapist who both suggested that perhaps Janine needed a higher level of care. Code for a program. Code for back to Whitman.

And maybe she did need that. This was no way to live. For any of us. When Janine was out with friends, I made her FaceTime me as she ate. It had to be humiliating. I didn't know what else to do.

Janine tried her best to complete three meals a day, a strategy she'd been assured by all the professionals would break the cycle of bingeing. It never did. One night, despite managing three solid meals, she texted me at midnight saying, *"I just binged again."*

I threw on my bathrobe and went downstairs. I sat on the couch with Janine. I took her head in my lap and combed her hair with my fingers. I heated up her rice sock. She says I sang her lullabies and that she didn't want me to stop. I don't remember that. It's possible. I was so exhausted.

The next morning, Janine refused to go to school again. These days she stayed home more than she made it to school despite our best efforts. She looked completely defeated.

"You can kick me out," she said, in a voice barely more than a whisper. "You can put me in a program. You can call DCF. I just don't care anymore." And I could see that it was true. Her affect was flat. Her voice lifeless. I could see that she just couldn't do it anymore. The bingeing. The restricting. We were trying so hard as a family, but here was our poor child miserable and hopeless, every day a struggle.

"I'll call Whitman today," I told her, rubbing her feet.

I couldn't see her face beneath her Medusa of curls, but the curls were nodding yes.

I was both relieved and disheartened to be back there. There was no adolescent binge eating disorder program so after another intake evaluation with labs, weight and EKG, Whitman recommended the adult partial hospitalization program. (Janine was almost 18 now.) We were disappointed. We had hoped for the program that specialized in binge eating disorder because it was an evening program and she could still go to school. Worse, the program they were recommending was a mix of anorexics and binge eaters and Janine feared being triggered to restrict.

But she tried.

The next day, I dropped her off at the program, breakfast, lunch and snacks all packed for her. As sad as I was about this setback and her missing school again, I was still comforted and relieved that the professionals were taking over her daytime care.

She started texting me before I even got home.

"Come pick me up. I can't do this."

"What's wrong?"

"They're only talking about anorexia. No one else here has a binge eating disorder."

This was everything we had feared. Still, I encouraged her to stay the day.

"When I come pick you up, let's sit down with staff and see if we can work something else out."

Janine ignored me.

"They made me measure my granola! It had to be just ¼ cup so they made me throw away some of what you packed for me! I'm not going back on a meal plan!"

This certainly did feel like a giant step backward. Janine had been making her own breakfast and lunch and serving herself dinner for such a long time. Yes, she binged sometimes and sometimes she couldn't resist the urge to restrict afterward. But we hadn't counted out almonds in over a year.

Whatever relief I had felt dropping Janine off that morning evaporated. I feared if this didn't work out, we'd be all alone and on our own again.

True to my word, I came early to pick Janine up and requested a meeting with the director, Bob. Janine and I made our case. The triggering bodies. The missing school. The dreaded meal plan. Janine was in tears. I was frustrated. Our reasoned pleas were met with a sympathetic face, earnestly nodding, but ultimately fell on deaf ears. Bob asked Janine to give it one more day. Come back Friday and on Monday we could re-convene.

Janine wasn't making any promises. She'd done what I asked and stayed the day. I doubted I'd be able to get her back there again.

Luckily, we had a therapy session with Rosie that very afternoon, so we headed right there after our disappointing meeting.

Rosie was outraged on our behalf. She agreed with us that the binge eating disorder program would have been a much better fit for Janine. She, too, felt that the partial program's environment would be triggering for Janine and that to go back on a meal plan was not only unnecessary but potentially harmful and a definite step back.

Janine felt vindicated. She and Rosie talked some more, then Janine signed a contract agreeing to go to school every day that week. She and Rosie would work on the binge eating together. We left there feeling much better. We had a plan.

And Janine kept her end of the bargain. She got herself up the next day, ate breakfast with me and went to school. I gave her an extra-long hug on her way out the door.

After she was gone, I dialed Whitman and asked for the director. I told him about our meeting with Rosie. How she agreed that the partial program wasn't right for Janine. How Janine had promised to eat breakfast and go to school and she did.

Bob seemed appreciative of Janine's efforts at the program the day before and also glad we weren't just taking things into our own hands without professional advice. He promised to inform DCF.

"I'll call them today," he said. "I'll tell them you made the decision in consultation with Janine's therapist."

"I appreciate that," I said sincerely.

"I'll get back to you with next steps after I hear from DCF," he concluded.

"Thanks," I said.

After school, Barb, the in-home counselor, asked Janine about her plans for the weekend.

"I'm going to a sleepover at my friend Emma's house," she reported with a smile. This was the first I was hearing about this.

"Who else is going?" I asked.

"Becca, Julia, and some girl Rhea I don't really know."

I was surprised. Janine had been invited to sleepovers at Emma's in the past which she had turned down after learning there'd be kids there she hadn't met. Janine had a lot of social anxiety and meeting new people was not her forte.

I was proud of her.

Proud for many reasons. I was proud of her for having insight into her own needs. Proud of her for advocating for herself in a room full of grown-ups at Whitman the day before. Proud of her for re-grouping and strategizing with Rosie around her ongoing binge eating. Proud of her for honoring her word and going to school. And now, proud of her for inching out of her comfort zone and making new friends. I went to bed with my heart brimming with love.

Sixteen

As Close to Death as This

That night, the night of the sleepover, Janine texted me at one in the morning.

I'm bleeding.

I thought she meant she had her period.

Ask Emma for a tampon.

No, I'm bleeding from my face.

I figured she had a nosebleed.

Put some ice on it, I advised. *It should stop. Do you want me to come get you?*

Idk.

Okay, well, let me know. Love you.

Love you too.

The *Idk* should have stopped me. I should have pushed a little harder to see how she felt. If she really wanted to come home but was hesitant to ask. Afraid to bother anyone. Instead, I went back to sleep.

An hour later, Saul got a call from Janine's phone. It was one of her friends saying she was having a seizure and was in an ambulance on her way to Clara Barton Hospital.

We threw on clothes and jumped in the car. I immediately started second-guessing myself. Did the nosebleed have something to do with the seizure? Had she had a seizure and fallen on her face? My mind was spinning faster than Saul's speeding wheels. I was awash in guilt. I should have brought her home.

In the emergency room, we were led by a nurse to Janine. As we walked, the nurse spoke with the on-call DCF social worker on her mobile phone, obtaining permission to treat. In her small cubicle, Janine lay on a stretcher, dressed in a johnnie, covered with a thin white sheet. She was hooked up to a heart monitor. An IV was in her right arm, a pulse oximeter on her right forefinger, so I positioned myself at her left side.

"Are you guys mad at me?" Janine's go-to worry. Abandonment. I smoothed her curls and kissed her forehead.

"No, my silly girl."

Janine smiled and closed her eyes. A nurse gave us an update. Her vital signs were stable, he assured us. The doctor would be in soon.

"She probably didn't even have a seizure," he added smugly. "She probably just passed out and got a little twitchy and her friends freaked out."

I resented his smugness, his dismissiveness. I thought of all the infants and toddlers I had cared for over the years who had had seizures after breath-holding spells. If Janine did pass out, she certainly could have become anoxic and seized. I didn't want to get into a pissing match with this nurse. I just wanted this taken seriously. I wanted a work-up. A CAT scan. Blood work. A tox screen. That's what I'd be ordering if this were my ER. But it wasn't.

The doctor came in and took a history first from Janine, then us. It turned out Emma's parents weren't home. It turned out there was drinking and smoking involved. It turned out there were boys. Janine admitted to drinking five vodka shots, which surprised me. She also smoked a lot of weed, which did not. She was a smoker but not a drinker that I knew of. Maybe I was just being naïve.

When it was our turn, we told the doctor about Janine's eating disorder, her depression, her anxiety, her meds.

"Did you take anything else, Janine?" the doctor prompted. "Anything at all?"

"No."

"Could someone have slipped you something?"

"I don't think so."

I was sitting at Janine's side, my hand on her left forearm when it suddenly started to twitch.

"I'm cold, Carolyn," Janine said, then her eyes rolled back in her head, lids fluttering madly. Her face turned a dusky purple. Her mouth clenched shut even as frothy white foam escaped from her lips. Her whole body convulsed.

"She's having another seizure!" I yelled. I stood up as the ER team flooded the room, backing me against a wall. I let them do their work.

A nurse wheeled in a red cart, opening drawers before it came to a stop. Another fitted Janine's blue face with an oxygen mask.

"Ativan 5," the doctor ordered, standing at the head of her bed.

Smug RN drew it up and injected it into her IV.

"Ativan 5 in," he reported back. I happened to glance up at the heart monitor. The previously orderly green blips marching across the screen had suddenly turned fast and wild.

"She's in V tach!" I screamed. Everyone who had previously been bent over my child suddenly jerked to attention, all our eyes on the now jagged arrhythmia.

"Amioderone 150," the doctor ordered. Smug RN pulled more code cart drawers open and delivered the drug efficiently, wrappers and med boxes cast aside.

"Amioderone 150 in," he reported.

Janine's body gradually calmed. Her rhythm normalized.

I was unnerved. I had seen many seizures in my work but never in a child of my own. I knew that she would come out of it. I knew we just had to find the cause. Watching her go into ventricular tachycardia was singularly terrifying. It was an unusual event in pediatrics, a rhythm that was often fatal if untreated. My own heart sank and my limbs grew heavy and cold as I suddenly realized that if I *had* brought Janine home, she may not have survived the night. I would have put her to bed and she would have gone into this fatal arrhythmia in her sleep. I would have gone into her room in the morning and found her dead in her bed. With all our close calls with Janine, with her suicidal gestures, her jumping out of cars, her starving herself for months and years, this was truly the closest to death she had ever been. My body shook uncontrollably. Tears ran down my face, unbidden.

I went back to Janine's side, holding her hand, rubbing her arm, pressing my cheek to her chest. Saul stood behind me. I took the hand he placed on my shoulder and turned to look at him. His face was white as a puff of smoke. This was my milieu and I felt helpless and overcome. He had to be a wreck.

"We're taking her to CAT scan now, Mom," the doctor informed me. I was glad they were finally ordering the study I'd wanted from the start. I knew it pained Saul to be separated from Janine. I also knew that between the seizure itself and the meds used to treat it, she'd be sleeping for a little while. She would be accompanied by trained medical staff.

When Janine was finally wheeled back to us, she was just starting to blink her eyes open.

"I'm cold," she said again. She was shaky. Her face was sweaty and flushed. Was that a side effect of the meds or due to whatever it was she had taken? (Because it was clear to me by now that she'd taken something.)

"I'll go get you a nice warm blanket," a nurse told her.

"Thank you," Janine said with a smile, her eyes closed.

The doctor came in and pronounced her brain scan normal.

"Obviously we'll be keeping her overnight," he added.

I thought about the smug nurse who didn't believe she'd had a seizure, the delayed brain scan, the V tach that only I had noticed.

"Or we could transfer her to Children's Hospital," I offered. He nodded and raised his eyebrows as if this were an idea worth considering.

"Or transfer to Children's," he agreed.

"That's what I want," I told him. He nodded solemnly. "It's where all her doctors are," I added. I didn't know if the nurses contacted DCF a second time or if they were letting me call the shots. I only know that my wishes were granted. We were being transferred to Boston.

Just like we had with Neil, I rode up front in the ambulance, Janine on a stretcher in back, while Saul followed behind us in his car. An EMT kept checking her vital signs and recording them on his metal clipboard. With each check, he gave me a thumbs up sign through the tiny square of glass that separated us. Those signs should have encouraged me, but I was shaky and scared. I held my head in my hands and cried.

At Children's Hospital, a huge team was waiting for us in full code blue mode. There was a scribe, ready to record what medications were given and at what time. A resident was verbally going through the ABCs of trauma: airway, breathing, circulation.

"Airway secure. Patient is breathing on her own. Well-saturated on room air."

I would gradually learn everyone's role. The ER attending was summarizing what was known so far.

"Seventeen-year-old female known to be on an SSRI, ingested alcohol and marijuana, then presented to an outside hospital having had a witnessed seizure and possible head injury. A second seizure was witnessed at the outside hospital and treated with five milligrams of Ativan. Patient then developed ventricular tachycardia treated with 150 milligrams of Amioderone. An additional five milligrams of Ativan was given en route in the ambulance for foot tremors. No further seizure activity was noted."

The toxicology fellow took over.

"Patient is flushed, tachycardic and diaphoretic, with ongoing tremors and increased muscle tone."

"I don't feel well," Janine said, eyes shut, trying to sit up. "I'm so shaky. Carolyn, where are you?"

I had been given a seat against the wall and was assigned my own nurse whose job it was to keep me informed of Janine's status. To interpret the doctors' words, though I needed no interpretation. She now touched my shoulder and motioned me toward the stretcher in the middle of the room. The nurse at the head of Janine's bed was trying to coax her to lie back down, but she only grew more agitated and restless, thrashing at her covers.

I bent my face to Janine's ear.

"Shh," I shushed gently. "It's okay. I'm here. Lie back down." Janine immediately calmed to my voice. I felt an intense pride at being the one to be able to soothe and reassure this child. The nurse nodded for me to stay where I was, near Janine. I rubbed her shoulder, wanting her to know I was near. I felt useful. I had a role here.

A cardiology fellow was also part of the team.

"The patient's SSRI could have interacted with another substance to produce her serotonergic symptoms. The working diagnosis is serotonin syndrome."

The words terrified me. Serotonin syndrome is a conglomeration of symptoms that occur when too much serotonergic medications, like the anti-depressants Janine was on, were in the body. Patients could spike temperatures of over 106 degrees, develop shakiness, seizures and muscle breakdown. There was no cure per se for serotonin syndrome. Treatment was just supportive. The doctors could treat her seizures and her arrhythmias but would basically just be waiting for the offending substance to leave her body.

People die from serotonin syndrome.

People die from V tach.

People die.

Janine was still with us.

A nurse soon led Saul into the room. His presence alone gave me a sense of relief. As scared as he was and helpless as he felt, he was still my rock. The toxicologist now turned to us.

"Do we know if the marijuana your daughter smoked was synthetic?" Saul and I were blank. "The synthetic cannabinoid K-2 is well known to have serotonergic properties." He was facing us, but his comments seemed meant for the team.

"Do we know what other meds might have been in the home?" he asked. We did not. I looked at the clock on the wall. It was five in the morning. Normally too early to start calling Janine's friends and their families. But this was literally life or death. Saul took his cell phone and went into the hall to try to find the information the doctors needed. He came back a short time later with the answer.

"Emma takes Celexa. They checked the bottle. It's empty."

———⊗⊗⊗———

Just as with Neil, we stayed with Janine throughout her ICU stay. There was a cushioned bench beneath a window and behind a curtain where parents could be near their children yet out of staff's way. Saul brought me changes of clothes every night when he came to visit. I told my business partner I needed the week off from work.

The conclusion her ICU team came to was that Janine had

overdosed on her friend's Celexa. We were awaiting blood levels of the drug, which was a send-out test and could take a few days. For now, that was the operating theory.

Janine wasn't buying it.

"We have no evidence that I took anything," she protested to the psychiatrist who came to evaluate her. "Why would I do that?" The psychiatrist was troubled that Janine seemed not to be taking any responsibility for her very reckless behavior. In a way, I could understand it. How do you begin to own something you can't recall? It worried me, too.

"Maybe I was feeling a little blue and took the pills to try to feel better," Janine conjectured. "Because I would never take them to try to kill myself."

That did not reassure anyone. What would happen the next time she was "feeling a little blue"? Would she be so dangerously impulsive again? Could Saul and I ever let her go to another sleepover? Could we ever leave her alone?

The psychiatrist recommended to the ICU team that when she was stable, Janine be transferred to an inpatient psychiatric unit for further observation and evaluation.

"I just want to go home," Janine complained to anyone who would listen. A familiar lament to us.

No one from DCF ever came to see Janine in the hospital. Behind the scenes they were very busy offering their opinion as to where they thought Janine should go. Their go-to recommendation? Clinton Care.

I couldn't understand DCF's reasoning. Both times Janine had tried to take her own life, DCF had tried to take her from us. Take from her the solidity and steadiness of family. Place her in the institution where she'd languished without cure. When we were her cure. At least her cure for abandonment and grief. Her cure for feeling alone and unsure. Ben had been right about one thing. Showing up for Janine day after day, time after time, advocating to remain her parents, had shown her our determined love more than any hug or words ever could.

This time we didn't have to advocate on our own. We didn't

contact lawyers or go up the chain of the DCF command. The doctors at Children's rejected DCF's recommendation. Instead they transferred us to an in-patient psychiatric facility. Once again we were admitted to the Thoreau Unit of Whitman Hospital. It was Whitman who had recommended their partial hospitalization program for Janine that had triggered her into this unhappy state that had led us here. And now it was Whitman that would receive her again.

We had come full circle.

In seventeen days.

SEVENTEEN

The Fight of Our Lives

"You made a very poor decision letting Janine go to that party," Rhonda, the DCF supervisor, was saying.

"It wasn't a party. It was a sleepover," I corrected her uselessly.

"She shouldn't have been let out of your house in that state," Janine's latest social worker Jessica added.

"What state?!" I yelled, then lowered my voice and continued. "She was in a great mood. She'd gone to school for the first time in forever. She'd made a contract with her therapist Rosie. Barb, the clinician *you guys* assigned us, had just seen her! *She* was aware of her plans. *She* didn't advise me to keep her home. Ask *her* about her state of mind." The decibels in my voice were creeping back up again.

We were seated around a conference table at Whitman Hospital planning for Janine's discharge. DCF was again gunning for Clinton Care. Jason, Whitman's social worker, agreed with us that Janine would be better served being home with intensive support services in place.

"It was an unsupervised party," DCF insisted.

"That wasn't known to any of us at the time," I maintained calmly. "It was a sleepover with five girls. Five good girls. Five straight-A girls. Girls whose houses Janine has slept at before. Girls whose parents I know." Despite having temporarily reined in my ire, I was again growing increasingly frustrated with their thinly veiled aspersions that I was a neglectful foster mother.

When we first became foster parents, DCF had told us magnanimously that they were not going to do their usual criminal background checks of homes that Janine frequented because they trusted our judgment so much. "Prudent parenting," they had called it. Now they were telling me my decisions were poor.

"Let's get back to the issue at hand," Jason said. The voice of reason. "When Janine heard that DCF was advocating for Clinton Care, she refused her meds for two days."

I hadn't known this. Had DCF? I looked over at Rhonda and Jessica. Their faces gave nothing away.

"The Bornsteins have provided the longest, most stable home Janine has known since she was removed from her mother's care." The workers nodded at this truth.

"It's home. It's her home," Jason continued.

Now Jessica and Rhonda exchanged glances. I tasted blood and realized I was biting the inside of my cheek.

"The department needs more time to determine what will serve Janine's needs best," Rhonda informed us all curtly. She was looking directly at Jason, seeming to avoid my eye. With a sudden sickening clarity, I knew what was happening here. They were going to take Janine away from us. Before I could take a breath and voice my fears, Jason took over.

"The department doesn't *have* more time. Her 30 days is over. Her insurance won't pay any more. Mass Health needs her discharged. Yesterday."

As if anticipating this development, Rhonda reached into her satchel and withdrew a sheaf of papers and slid them over to Jason who began reading.

"The department wants her transferred to Hill House."

"Wait. What's Hill House?" I asked, panicked. Another Clinton Care? A group home where they could let Janine languish until she aged out of foster care?

"It's a TCU," Jason answered distractedly, his eyes on the paperwork in front of him.

"What's a TCU?" I asked.

"Sorry. Transitional care unit," Jason explained.

"It will give us more time to evaluate Janine. Decide when she's ready to live in the community." Rhonda with her euphemisms.

I was angry. DCF was playing with all our lives here.

"This was a very serious event, Carolyn," Rhonda declared.

That was the last straw. I stood up.

"Don't tell me about serious events, Rhonda," I seethed. "She had a seizure right in front of me, for Christ's sake. She went into V tach before my eyes. She could have died. *I* was the one who slept next to her bed the entire time she was in the hospital. You were not there. *I* was. So don't lecture me about how serious an event this was."

I sat down heavily. No one immediately reacted.

"It's close to you," Jason finally said.

"What?" I asked.

"Hill House. It's in the next town over from you," Jason said.

"She can keep going to high school. The department will arrange transportation," Rhonda informed us.

My panic receded a tiny bit. Maybe I had read things wrong. Maybe DCF wasn't trying to take her away from us.

"Can we visit her?" I ventured.

"We can consider a visitation schedule." Nothing could be just yes or no with Rhonda.

"This seems like a compromise for DCF, Dr. Bornstein," Jason said. "It's not Clinton Care and it buys everyone more time."

I didn't need more time. I needed my child. Home. Now. But it seemed like Jason was telling me to take what I was being offered. So I did. As if I had a choice.

———

That night, as I was cleaning the kitchen after dinner, I got a phone call from Jessica, Janine's social worker. The caller ID just read DCF. Her social workers changed so often I didn't even bother to add their names anymore.

"A 51-A has been filed against your family," she said robotically. My mouth went dry. My heart sank into my stomach.

"What?" I asked. "By whom?"

"A 51-A has been filed against your family," she repeated, then went on. "I know you were going to take Janine to see her nurse practitioner this week, but you'll have to cancel that appointment," she added.

"Why?" I stammered. I was confused and afraid.

"A member of the department must be present at all medical visits," she informed me.

I couldn't fathom what was happening. A second 51-A. I hung up the phone before she could say another word.

Saul came into the kitchen.

"What's happening?"

Rhonda's words from earlier that day came back to me. "You made a very poor decision letting her go to that party."

"I think DCF just filed a 51-A on us," I said. It was the only conclusion I could reach that made any sense. It had been almost three weeks since Janine had been hospitalized for the seizure. If any staff at either Children's or Whitman had thought us neglectful for letting Janine go to a party, they would have filed on us long ago. A mandated reporter has 48 hours after a suspicious incident to file charges. I filed 51-As routinely in my line of work and you don't wait three weeks.

It was also insane. I had taken care of many intoxicated teenagers in the emergency room, uncovered countless cases of substance abuse in my office. Not once did it ever occur to me to blame the parents and file a 51-A. I got the family into therapy. Offered substance abuse counseling for the teen. Accusing the parents of neglect was just not part of my practice. Obviously, it was not part of Children's or Whitman's either.

Saul and I just held each other, too stunned to speak.

There had been a recent spate of deaths of children in DCF custody in Massachusetts, three in short succession, prompting our new governor to redefine and narrow the department's mission. While the previous mission had been two-pronged—keep kids safe and keep families together—the governor changed the mission to simply "keep kids safe."

Janine had very nearly died. On DCF's watch. In their view, I'm sure someone had to be held accountable for not keeping their charge safe. So they were blaming me. Again I thought back to the meeting. Is this what DCF needed more time for? To file a 51-A? To wait for the investigator to support the allegation as the proof of neglect they needed to take Janine away? Permanently?

I waited day after day for a phone call from the investigator. Every day ended with no communication. I was terrified. DCF had already screened out one 51-A against us. Would they dismiss this one too? It took nearly two anxiety-ridden weeks for the investigator to call and set up a time to meet. When she finally came, my fears redoubled. She did not seem to have the same concern as Rhonda about us letting Janine go to an unsupervised sleepover. Instead she focused on my "lack of communication" with DCF. As examples, she brought up the fact that I had not told DCF directly when I took Janine out of Whitman's partial program and allegedly failed to inform anyone in the department when she was hospitalized.

"DCF *was* informed," I protested. "I heard the nurse talk to them myself."

"*You* never called," the investigator told me, peering over her bifocals.

"Janine's social worker called me at the hospital the next day so clearly she got the message."

The investigator made no response.

"And the director of Whitman himself told me he'd tell DCF Janine wasn't coming back to the program. He said he'd let me know what they wanted to do next."

The investigator kept writing. She did not look up at me, so I continued on, desperate to make my case.

"He even said he'd tell them … tell *you* … tell DCF … that I hadn't made the decision alone. That Janine's therapist had recommended she not go back." I would learn much later that, although Bob did put in a call to DCF about Janine's withdrawal from the program at Rosie's recommendation, no one from DCF ever called him back.

The investigator shut her notebook. I couldn't read her look. I swear she hadn't blinked once through the whole interview.

"We'll be in touch, Mrs. Bornstein," she said. With that, she stood and let herself out the door. I felt like someone had quietly slipped all the bones out of my body. Like there was nothing at all holding me up.

I waited day after day to hear the results of the investigation. It was difficult to concentrate at work. I slept poorly. To be accused of neglect for a second time felt shameful, even though I knew in my heart I was being the best foster mother I could be. That I was the best person to care for both my girls. To have my mothering questioned, to be accused of being a neglectful parent cut me to the core of who I was. More than any other role, being a mother was how I defined myself. It was my most important job. More than doctor, or writer, or speaker, being a mom was everything to me. And now, how I performed that central role was being attacked. The whole process was deeply soul-crippling. No matter how it turned out—whether the allegation was supported or dismissed—I was personally totally demoralized.

Janine went to Hill House. The school transportation that DCF was supposed to arrange never materialized. It was just as well. Every day, either Saul or I would pick her up in the morning and take her to Newburyport High School, then fetch her in the afternoon and bring her back to the group home. At first, we were only allowed to visit for two hours on the weekends, and even then, we were not allowed to take her back to our house. So we went for walks in nearby salt marshes or on Trustees of the Reservation land or just out for ice cream at Dairy Queen.

Janine begged us to take her home. "I just want to lie in my bed," she pleaded. "I just want to pet my cats."

We were not on solid ground here. We couldn't break any rules.

On the morning of the meeting at which we would learn whether DCF would send Janine back to Clinton Care or let her come home to her family, the investigator called to tell us that she was finding in our favor. The 51-A was, again, unsupported. She still needed to pass it by her supervisor, but she assured us that that was just a formality.

"I know you have a meeting today. Feel free to use this information," she told us. "And good luck," she added kindly.

Saul and I held each other in the middle of the kitchen floor for a long while. This is where it had started. Where I first told Saul about two strong sad girls who needed us. Where he had said, *Tell DCF yes.* Where I had gotten both phone calls informing us about the 51-As.

And this is where it would end.

Relief was not the right word to describe how we felt. Yes, it was good to no longer have the investigation hanging over our heads as it had all these weeks. Yes, we felt vindicated. But damaged, too. Our faith in the bureaucracy that still had control over two of our children had been badly shaken.

The meeting at Hill House was filled with DCF workers. Each social worker had a supervisor and each supervisor had a manager. There were people there I had never met before. When we were all assembled and formally introduced, they brought Janine in. I had never seen her look so down. Her shoulders slumped, her head bowed. Her chin hit her chest. Her face was covered with unbrushed hair. She sat down next to me, air escaping her in a long sigh. She leaned on my shoulder.

"Please make them let me come home, Carolyn," she said from under her hair, her voice barely a whisper. "I can't stay here anymore."

I pressed my lips to the top of her head.

"I know, my girl," I whispered to Janine.

"I just can't," she said again.

Something shifted in me just then. I'm not sure I can say even now just what it was. Maybe it was the way she said the word home. Like a longed-for but far-away solace. Maybe it was the way her defeated body leaned against mine, seeking shelter. Maybe it was something about facing that room full of professionals whose job it was to care for Janine, to provide for her. Or the firm knowledge that I was the one who knew her best and loved her most.

If we weren't a family before, we became one in that moment. Committed as blood. I had always told the girls I would never leave them. Now I also knew this. They would never leave me either. I understood that that decision was technically out of my control. That DCF could re-home kids with no notice and little cause. I knew then and there I would never let that happen. Whatever happened here today, whatever decision DCF would make—to let Janine come home with us or send her back to Clinton Care—we would always fight to keep Janine and Mariah. In that moment I knew. This was their last stop on the struggle bus.

EIGHTEEN

Doubling Down on Love

Janine was finally allowed to come home with us from Hill House. DCF never tried to separate her from us again. She eventually overcame her eating disorder, or at least tamed it to a manageable animal. The pendulum that had swung so wildly for so long—years toward starvation, months toward excess—finally quieted. Like a stillpoint. No rushing toward one or racing from the other. Just done.

There was no moment of epiphany. No one successful therapy, one brilliant strategy that worked. Just the quiet of a fever breaking, or the ragged breath of a toddler whose tantrum is wrung out. Her eating disorder is still there, of course; Edie lurking like a dormant virus in a nerve, ready to be triggered awake to do its damage if allowed. A reservist waiting to be called up.

Mariah is back home now, too. Her apartment with her boyfriend didn't work out. Neither did the one she later shared with a friend. Both times she decided that her home was really our home. And both times we took her back gladly; the warp and weft of family life now firmly intertwined.

Foster children, when they turn 18 and age out of the system, have few options if they have not been found a permanent placement by DCF. The statistics are grim. Twenty percent will be instantly homeless. Seven out of ten girls who age out will become pregnant by the age of 21. There is a less than a 3 percent chance that a child who has aged out of foster care will earn a college degree in their lifetime.

Even with support, figuring out the future is hard when the past has been so troubled. Janine dropped out of high school before getting her GED and completing an Emergency Medical Technician course. Mariah started college but quickly got overwhelmed and abandoned her studies. Now she is back on track, working as a pharmacy technician and accepted into a four-year state university. I am so proud of both of them. Where would they be if they had to be on their own? If they had no one to push them a little and say, "You can do this. I believe in you"? No one to catch them when they fall?

"We're still catching our children," a friend told me over lunch one day as we discussed our grown kids. And it's true. We carry them on our health insurance for as long as we can. We keep them on our cell phone plans. We co-sign loans for them as young adults.

That's what I want for my kids. For all of them. To know they have a place to come home to if they hit a rough patch in life. I want them to come back home for Thanksgiving dinner. I want their kids to have sleepovers with Nana and Papa, to wake up here on Christmas morning.

I've often thought about what it was that drew me to these girls in the first place. I had cared for thousands of patients over the years in similar distress without calling the Department of Children and Families to say, *Let me help.* I had watched foster kids get shuffled from home to home, program to program before without being so moved as to come home and ask my husband, *Can we take them? Can we make them ours?*

And why now? When most of my friends were retiring and traveling, why was I instead choosing to meet with social workers, get background-checked and start mothering teens all over again?

I like to think I came forward for benevolent reasons. I saw a wrong I wanted to right. Potential going untapped. Two strong girls floundering under the weight of dire circumstances. Maybe I was also trying to apologize. To Jimmy. For not doing more for him at the end of his life. To Linda. For not trying harder to keep her family intact. To the girls themselves for not seeing the domestic violence and relentless inebriation that defined their childhood. As their pediatrician, I will carry that guilt with me always. Information that came out, not in my exam room, but in dribs and drabs over months and years. In family therapy sessions and late night mother-daughter talks.

Maybe I was trying to apologize to my own children, too. I was in medical school when our boys were small. I felt guilty for all the long hours I spent away from them at the library, memorizing the names of tendons and bones, the Krebs Cycle, oxidative phosphorylation. When I was with them, snug on their top bunk with snacks and toys and pretend fishing poles playing "shipwrecked," I was distracted, sure that I would fail anatomy. Flunk out of medical school altogether. That every one of my classmates was studying at that very moment except me.

During my residency, Saul would bring the boys to visit me when I was on call. We'd watch movies in my call room, the tapes and portable VCR player borrowed from the Play Lady on the pediatric ward. In the summer, we'd eat hamburgers on picnic benches outside the emergency room, watching the Life Flight helicopters take off and land from the helipad nearby. Dan and Neil have told me they have fond memories of those times. But my absence from their young lives still haunts me. I wonder if I was around enough during their seminal years.

So compelling is my fear that, from time to time, even now, I still pore over boxes of photographs asking the small round faces looking back at me from the pile, *Was I there for you? Was I enough?* Until finally, page after page of photos—decorating dinosaur birthday cakes together, pulling snow-suited boys over snow in wooden apple carts bungeed to sleds, black-and-white stills of Mommy and Me music classes—would finally calm my fears, convince me that *yes, I was there.*

Until the next time that the doubts creep in.

Life is lived forward but understood backwards, a philosopher once said. I could not have predicted how changed and full and blessed my life would be at this point by bringing these girls into it. "You knew what you were getting into when you took us in!" Janine shouted at me once in the middle of a fight. The truth is I didn't. None of us know what we are getting into when we choose to become parents. Back when we first made the decision to foster, Saul and I thought it was us who were gambling here. Opening up our comfortably empty nest to two new and needy girls. Putting off a retirement that seemed just around the corner. Committing to the unknown, no pre-nups in parenthood.

Now I understand that it was these sisters who had taken the bigger chance on us. Opening themselves up to further loss and abandonment. After everything they had been through. After being deserted—intentionally or not—by everyone they had ever known or loved. After the death of their father. After their mother could no longer care for them. After eleven foster homes in five years, they still had enough faith to take a chance on us. To risk everything. Betting it all on strangers. And doubling down on love.

Epilogue

Janine stopped walking and clutched the railing on the wall. I stepped behind her and rubbed her lower back in small slow circles. She breathed in slowly through her nose and out through her mouth like she had learned in pre-natal yoga.

"That's it. You're doing great. One more contraction under your belt."

Her breath slackened. Her eyes slowly opened. She gave herself a little satisfied nod and we continued walking. We were a team. Janine in the middle. Me and Cameron on either side. Taking turns holding her up, rubbing her back, saying encouraging words.

She had been in labor for more than 24 hours now. She had sent me a picture at work the day before.

"This came out of my vagina!" she texted, so characteristically unselfconscious.

It was her mucus plug. So I knew labor wouldn't be far behind. Sure enough, I had woken at 6 a.m. to Janine sitting at the kitchen table with Saul.

"I think I'm in labor."

And she was. I put my hand on her belly, feeling it tighten at regular intervals. We added some toiletries to her pre-packed bag and waited for Cameron to arrive. Saul left for work and Cam, Janine and I drove to the hospital. We checked into the labor and delivery suite, only to be sent home by the midwife as she was only two centimeters dilated.

Now, a day later, she was five. Just making that much progress had boosted Janine's confidence and she was walking and breathing through contractions with quiet determination.

"You're doing great," I whispered. "You're really good at this."

"I am?" she asked after her contraction had passed. I smiled and nodded.

———∝◦⊷———

Mariah joined us at nine in the morning. She was dressed for work in her blue pharmacy scrubs. Janine had texted her when she was getting close to delivering, so she had left work and now she sat by Janine's head smoothing her curls, silently supportive.

As the morning wore on, Janine's contractions grew closer and stronger. Now instead of just breathing through them, her body wanted to moan.

"Good work," I whispered during each one. "You're doing great." Mariah and Cameron were happy to let me take the lead in coaching. I'd seen so many babies born, so many women in labor. Janine was doing better than any I'd witnessed.

I knew to keep quiet. I knew how hard it was to concentrate in labor. How every stray word distracted. It took Cam a while to figure that out. Janine had even devised a shorthand for "I need quiet." When Cam started chattering nervously, she lifted her hand above her head, keeping her eyes closed, and snapped her fingers shut like an alligator's mouth. A silent "zip it!"

When Janine felt like pushing, the nurse and the midwife positioned her in bed. Mariah stayed at her sister's side. I looked at their painted fingernails, intertwined pink and blue, holding each other's hands. I thought of them going off to the salon together before Janine's first day of high school. Now Janine was about to be a mother. Mariah, an aunt. I thought about how much they had been through together. I saw them as little girls in my office: Mariah sick and pale, Janine wide-eyed and afraid. Now they were grown young women, one bringing new life into the world. One stalwartly by her side.

My eyes welled up.

I thought about their mom, too mentally ill to be here for Janine. Too wrapped up in her own sick perseverations to even clearly register her daughter's pregnancy. I thought of Jimmy and how proud he would be of both his girls. How he would be here if he could.

Was, in a way. I wiped my tears before the girls could see them. I didn't want to take attention away from Janine's monumental task at hand.

Soon a patch of dark wet hair appeared.

"There she is, Janine. Look down," Cam said excitedly. But Janine was absorbed. With each contraction, she took a deep inspiration, relaxed her perineum and pushed from deep within herself. She had been good at labor and she was going to be good at delivery. Some women never got the hang of pushing, never figured out how to relax their birth canal muscles, instead screaming through contractions and pushing ineffectively even after the tightening had passed. Not my Janine. She was at one with her body. Sensing what was happening inside her. Knowing instinctively what to do in response.

The nurse was gently turning Janine onto her left side. She placed Janine's right leg in my arms.

"Pulling up during contractions will help push the baby out," she told me. I nodded.

Her contractions were almost continuous now. Janine's face contorted with concentration and effort with each one. Her focus singular and aimed straight.

"I'm so proud of you." I continued my mantras. "You're doing great. She's almost here." My voice was the only one in the room. Even the midwife was silent now, letting me do all the coaching. Janine would occasionally nod in reply. Mostly she kept her eyes closed and pushed.

Cameron relieved me at Janine's right leg. Mariah took Cam's position at the bottom of the bed, watching the birth over the midwife's shoulder. I stayed at Janine's head, changing the cool washcloth on her forehead, kissing her temples, arranging her sweaty curls around her face.

"Play with my hair," she used to tell me when she was younger. I swallowed hard, trying to stay present.

"Her head is out. I need you to just breathe, Janine. Just breathe. Don't push," the midwife instructed, expertly suctioning the baby's nose and mouth with a blue plastic bulb syringe.

"Look down, Janine, look down," Cameron pleaded, desperate to share his wonder. Mariah just watched, quietly absorbed in this miracle playing out before her.

In the next moment, the baby's body slid from her mother's. Her wet eyes were wide and searching. Her skin a dusky blue. She lifted her arms, catching sight of her own hands as they passed in front of her face. She was perfect.

The nurse went to work. She laid the infant on her mother's chest and rubbed her vigorously with clean white towels.

"Hi, beautiful girl," Janine cooed at her daughter.

"C'mon, cry," the nurse implored under her breath.

"She's fine," I said quietly. Maybe to myself. Maybe aloud. This baby wasn't crying but she certainly was fine. I saw it in her piercing eyes, her reaching hands. I thought I'd be the opposite, detecting pathology, sensing danger. A doctor-grandma worrywart. But here I was, calmly knowing all was well, even as the nurse whisked her charge frantically onto the infant warmer.

"C'mon, cry."

Even as no cries filled the air.

"Is she okay?" Janine called to the nurses, for now there were two, the second summoned by the first. No one answered Janine.

"She's perfect," I told her confidently.

Finally, a tiny squeak erupted from the infant.

"I guess that'll have to do," the nurse begrudged, wrapping the small still body in a blanket and placing her in Janine's arms. Janine and Cam smiled the wondrous, stupefied smiles of brand-new parents. They folded down the edges of the blanket to see more of their child, touching her nose, her cheeks, to make her real.

Mariah's face looked reverent as she watched her new niece, still in her sister's arms. As usual, Mariah was quiet, keeping her thoughts and feelings to herself. As was so often the case, part of her was impenetrable.

The baby made the rounds. Her daddy held her first. Then Auntie Mariah.

"Do you want to hold her, Carolyn?" Janine finally asked.

193

Epilogue

She placed the baby in my arms. I inhaled her scent, fresh from her mother's womb. I was aware of the others in the room. Our team. My family. I vaguely heard their voices as they shared each other's accounts of the minutes and hours just past. My world narrowed to the tiny girl before me. The eyes of her mother. The nose of her aunt.

"Hi, my girl," I whispered and kissed her. "It's Nana."

Index